Life, Love, and the In-Between:

A Geriatrician's Journey Through Aging and the Meaning of Life

Golnosh Sharafsaleh, MD, MS, MBA, DipABLM, FAAFP, AGSF

© 2025 Golnosh Sharafsaleh. All rights reserved.

No part of this book may be reproduced, stored in a retrieval system, or transmitted in any form
or by any means, electronic, mechanical, photocopying, recording, or otherwise, without prior written permission of the author, except for brief quotations used in reviews or scholarly analysis.

Published by Mosaic Path Press
Asheville, NC

ISBN: 979-8-9940146-0-8 (Hardcover)

First Edition: 2025

This book is intended for educational and informational purposes only.
It is not a substitute for professional medical advice, diagnosis, or treatment.
Readers should consult their own healthcare professionals regarding individual health concerns.

Printed in the United States of America.

Cover design by Mosaic Path Press
Interior design by Mosaic Path Press

For my family — for Jas, Mila, Zoey, and Peyton —
for James, whose brief life changed mine forever,
and for my patients, who continue to teach me how to live in the in-between,
you are the heart of this book.

Out of respect for my patients and their families, I have changed names and identifying details. The stories remain true, but the identities are protected.

Table of Contents

Introduction —The Journey Begins 6

Chapter 1 — James and the Fragility of Life 10

Chapter 2 — The Power of Love 31

Chapter 3 — The In-Between: Making the Moments Matter 43

Chapter 4 — The Truth Matters: How Transparency and Honesty Transform Patient Care 56

Chapter 5 — Compassion in Practice: The Universal Power of Empathy.................... 72

Chapter 6 — Creating Your Own Life Without Expectations 90

Chapter 7 — The Spirit's Triumph: Navigating Life's Trials with Strength and Hope... 107

Chapter 8 — Adapting and Embracing Change 126

Chapter 9 — Learning From Loss 148

Chapter 10 — Relevance 165

Chapter 11 — The Full Circle and the Big Picture 182

Epilogue... 201

Acknowledgements 207

Books That Inspire Growth............................... 209

Introduction
The Journey Begins

Life is a series of moments strung together, each one adding to the tapestry of our existence. Some bring joy, others sorrow, and many fall somewhere in between. *Life, Love, and the In Between* is a reflection on these moments, the lessons learned through both triumphs and tragedies, and the transformative power of love.

In 2016, I stood before an audience at a women's conference and shared a deeply personal story: the story of my son, James, who was born with a congenital heart defect and destined to live a brief, yet profoundly meaningful life. On the day of his birth, we cried tears of joy as we welcomed him into a world of unknowns. A photographer, herself a mother who had once lost a child, volunteered her time to capture his first moments. Through her lens, she preserved James's small but powerful cry, his gray eyes, his light brown hair, all of it filling our hearts with wonder and love.

James weighed just four pounds, a tiny, premature baby, yet full of life and spirit. Knowing our time with him would be short, we embraced every moment. We took him to the park, the bar, on hayrides, we made every day count. The audience at the conference didn't know how James's story would end until I shared, at the conclusion of my talk, that he had passed away at just eight weeks old. The room fell silent, then tears began to flow. Though it was painful to speak about James so soon after his passing, I felt compelled to share his story.

Through James's journey, I began to understand the meaning of *the in between*—the space between birth and death. Every moment mattered. Every experience was sacred. And love was the thread that held it all together. That understanding only deepened as I continued my work as a geriatrician, walking alongside my patients during the final chapters of their lives. Each encounter has offered profound lessons on living, loving, and navigating the in between.

This book continues that journey. It expands on the themes I first spoke about in that room years ago, weaving together stories from my patients, stories that have taught me what it means to live with purpose and to die with dignity. Each chapter explores a different facet of life, drawn from real experiences that reveal truths about the human spirit.

You will read about the fragility of life, the power of love, the importance of presence, and the necessity of transparency in care. You'll see how compassion, resilience, and meaningful connection shape our experiences, and how understanding the whole person is essential in providing true care. In the final chapter, I invite you to reflect with me on life's ultimate meaning and the legacy we leave behind.

I often reflect on my own imperfections, how I could be a better doctor, a more patient mother, a more understanding wife, daughter, sister. As a human being, I struggle with this deeply. And yet, my patients constantly remind me of what truly matters. I've come to believe that this is part of the journey: we fail, and we fail again. But somehow, tucked within those failures are the very treasures that shape us. They become the lessons we carry forward, the ones that help us grow into who we are meant to be.

I felt called to write this book because in our culture, the wisdom of our elders is too often overlooked. As a geriatrician, I am fortunate, not to have only one parent or grandparent sharing their wisdom, but many. Each patient has given me more than I could ever give them. This book is my way of honoring them.

My hope is that within these stories, you'll find comfort, insight, and a renewed appreciation for the moments that so often go unnoticed. Life isn't just about the beginning or the end, it's about the richness of what lies between. The love we give and receive, the lessons we learn, and the people who shape us along the way.

As we begin this journey together, I invite you to open your heart to these stories, to the wisdom of my patients, the experiences that shaped them, and the quiet, powerful beauty of life in the in between.

Dear Reader, One last note about this book, and about my words. I used to write to escape. In high school, I took creative writing classes and even enrolled in courses at the Salt

Lake Community College. I wrote poetry back then, and once even won a poetry contest.

If you notice the occasional poetic turn in my writing, I hope it doesn't distract from the true intention of this book.

Chapter 1

James and the fragility of Life

Life is a delicate dance between fragility and strength. We are frequently seduced by the illusion of control, believing that we can shape our destinies with our plans and decisions. Yet, the universe threads its own patterns, reminding us of our vulnerability and the inevitable moments when we crumble. Time flows relentlessly, a river that carries us forward, urging us to embrace each moment with open arms. In the face of our fragility, there lies the opportunity to savor life's beauty, to live boldly, and to exit with grace and dignity.

James was born on a cool day just before spring, March 9th, 2016. He arrived, beautiful and tiny, weighing a mere 4 lb. On that day, James was greeted by his grandparents, aunts, cousins, and his sister. We were aware of his terminal diagnosis, prepared to greet him for what might be mere minutes, perhaps hours at best—days, no one could predict, but prepared to both say hello and goodbye.

I longed to know you, to understand you, to hold you close, to breathe in your essence fully. Fear gripped me, fear of the unknowns that lay ahead. Until then, my life had followed a meticulously planned path. I knew I would become a doctor, marry, train as a resident, specialize in geriatrics, and raise my children. My life's calendar seemed so neatly arranged, each day a steppingstone toward a known future. How naive I was, how foolishly certain that I could control every outcome. In my 37 years, why had I not yet learned that despite our plans, we are never truly in control? Even as I calculated and rearranged my life calendar when things didn't go exactly as planned, I still felt as though I had complete control of the present and future.

Did it take James's fragile breath and eventual passing to teach me this profound lesson? I wonder now, did God need to send such a loud and painful message for me to understand? How could a loving God allow such cruelty—to bless us with a seemingly perfect child who appeared healthy on the outside, yet bore a broken heart within? The decisions I faced during my pregnancy, the choices that awaited us upon his birth, each one weighed heavily, testing my understanding of fate and faith alike.

James was born via C-section, my third one. I had complete placenta previa, meaning his placenta was positioned low, making a vaginal birth impossible. Throughout my pregnancy, I was warned that any bleeding could signal a life-threatening emergency. One night, I woke to use the bathroom, and when I stood up, it was as if a glass full of blood had spilled onto the floor. The rush was startling, more than just a trickle—it soaked the bathroom tiles in an instant. I woke my husband, urging him to stay with our daughters, Mila and Zoey, as I rushed to the hospital, despite medical advice against it. The stubbornness of doctors, even when it comes to their own health, is a well-known irony.

At the hospital, they urged me to stay on bed rest, cautioning that another bleed could be fatal. But how could I stay? I had a family to care for. Mila was five, Zoey just three. My husband was in his third year of fellowship in pulmonary critical care, and I was balancing my role as a geriatrician and family physician. The medical community understood the gravity of my situation, a fellow physician expecting a child destined to die. They explained the risks, but the urgency of my responsibilities as a mother and wife overshadowed everything else. As a physician myself, I understood all too well the protocol, they would have to document my departure against medical advice, something I had often charted myself when patients chose to leave against my recommendations. Luckily, no more bleeding until James was born.

As physicians, we learn perseverance through adversity. When Zoey my middle child was born, Jas (pronounced Jase) had to begin his fellowship, leaving me to care for a newborn and a toddler while completing my own fellowship. I remember the challenges vividly, the reopened c-section scar, daily packing, and relentless hospital duties. Becoming a doctor isn't just a profession; it's a path marked by failures, heartaches, sleepless nights, and constant fears. Becoming a physician is a journey that transforms us into a unique breed of humans.

I was around 18 weeks pregnant and going for my anatomy ultrasound, the moment when you can get a nice close-up look at the baby. I was so excited. In the past, I was in medical training and didn't have time to enjoy pregnancy like other first-time mothers. I had to rush to an ultrasound or an appointment in between caring for patients since I was an intern and a second-year resident for my first pregnancy, and a Geriatric fellow for my second pregnancy. This time was different; I was going to enjoy this pregnancy, planning, reflecting, and loving rather than trying to fit a baby into the grueling schedule of medical training. I had time. I felt an overwhelming sense of joy and anticipation. The thought of feeling those first gentle kicks, planning the nursery, and imagining the future as a family of five filled me with happiness.

Since I was considered to be a geriatric pregnancy, having been pregnant after the age of 35, I had done genetic testing early on. We knew we were going to have a boy and were told that James did not have any of the common genetic disorders they were testing for. This added to my excitement and reassurance. I called my mother-in-law, Debbie, whom I call Mom, and asked her to join me. This would be the first time she would get to be there for an ultrasound.

As the sonographer started to take pictures, she suddenly got up and walked out of the room. A few minutes later, the radiologist came in to discuss the abnormalities they had noticed on the scan. I remember her saying, "Golnosh, the apex of your baby's heart is pointed to the right." I stared at her surprised, the heart should be pointed to the left, but rarely major organs can have a reverse position called situs inversus. This doesn't necessarily mean anything is wrong, just different. I then asked her where the other organs were, and she proceeded to say the other major organs were where they would normally be. I stared at the radiologist, confused. "Your baby's heart doesn't seem to have developed properly. There are really no left-sided heart structures. Oxygenated and deoxygenated blood is pooling into a common chamber," she said.

I stared at her in disbelief.

My back was turned to my mother-in-law, and I didn't dare turn around so she could see my face. I was told that I needed to see a pediatric cardiologist within the next two weeks and have better imaging studies of my baby boy's heart. Shocked, I managed to walk out of that room and up to the front desk to check out. Somehow, my head was still turned so that my mom could not see my face. I started to wipe my face as tears started rolling down my cheeks. The receptionist knew me, I used to cover and moonlight at the urgent care in that building. We looked at each other, her eyes locked onto mine, she knew I wasn't ok, she knew and understood as she quickly tried to arrange an appointment with the cardiologist. I tried to keep my cool until we got home. But on the inside, I couldn't focus. I felt like I was suffocating, like the walls were closing in around me. I felt defeated, overwhelmed by a wave of despair that I couldn't escape.

Once home, I sat on the couch for what felt like many hours, just staring at the ceiling. How, I thought, there must be a mistake. It has to be okay. But the words "your baby does not have left-sided heart structures" kept playing in my head. What the hell, I thought, how can this be possible? I have planned every moment of my life. I planned for this pregnancy, eating the right things, doing the right things, I was healthy. I kept telling myself there must be a mistake.

Jas came home in the evening, and I told him everything I was told. I was tearful, and my eternally optimistic husband said that it would be okay. To wait until we saw the cardiologist and try not to worry. How could I not worry, I thought. I saw his worry; he didn't look so relaxed, and yet he was trying to comfort me. He didn't want me to hurt. Wow, I thought, this man really doesn't want me to stress, and here, right now, there is nothing he can do to take away the pain that I feel at the pit of my gut, the anger, fear, and confusion.

It took two weeks before we could be seen by a pediatric cardiologist. Those two weeks felt like a decade, and finally, I found myself in the waiting room of the pediatric cardiologist's office. Pediatric cardiac patients were running around and playing, while mine was still in my belly. Jas had to work, but he met me there. More ultrasound goop, more looking, more silence as we waited for the cardiologist to come into the room. More goop, more looking as the cardiologist instructed the sonographer to move her probe from one end of my stomach to another. More confusion, and then we were directed to an exam room. I wanted to throw up; I knew the news was going to be bad.

As the cardiologist started to draw a picture of James's heart, I knew exactly what he was saying. My husband had also done his own research over the last two weeks and completely grasped the situation. Interestingly, Jas and I had not discussed what we were researching, but as two physicians, we knew how to find the articles we needed and how to analyze what we were reading. As two doctors who had not heard of this rare diagnosis, we had the tools to figure it out. Everything I read over the last two weeks led to the diagnosis of heterotaxy. I guess my sweet husband had come to the same conclusion.

We were told that our baby would have severe defects and that the only possible treatment approaches would be palliative surgical treatments to help divert oxygenated blood, but he would be sick. He would need a heart transplant if he survived, and the chances of survival were poor. He would live with symptoms of heart failure and developmental delay. Everything Jas and I had read was being spoken in this room. It was out in the open, and it was going to happen.

The cardiologist provided us with two options: travel to one of the handful of hospitals in the country with experience handling this condition, where James could be delivered with the best chance of survival, or terminate our pregnancy. We were only about 20 weeks pregnant at this time, and he said termination of pregnancy was an option.

I asked the cardiologist how James was doing now. From what I had read, he wouldn't have any breathing issues until he was born since he was getting everything he needed from the umbilical cord. The cardiologist confirmed my assessment. He said without medical interventions, James would have only days, weeks, to months to live. I cried, Jas cried. I walked out of the room, to my car, and cried all the way home. I cried so much I couldn't see the road clearly; I was hyperventilating, screaming, and hitting the steering wheel with the palms of my hands. I screamed at God, telling Him how fucked up this was. I'm not sure exactly how I made it home, but I did. Poor Jas had to go back to work. He had to go back and pretend that he wasn't just told that his unborn son had a terminal medical diagnosis.

When I was asked about terminating the pregnancy, I was taken aback, but as a physician, I understood why the question was raised. Had this been my first pregnancy, with all the complications I faced, it likely would have been my last. But this was my third pregnancy. I knew James was not suffering, and I chose to continue. Over the years, I've grown deeply frustrated with our political system, with people attempting to dictate what women should or shouldn't do with their bodies. These are decisions that must remain between a physician and their patient, because the right choice is never the same for everyone, it changes depending on the circumstances and stage of life. What's needed is understanding and empathy. Doctors should be able to guide and support their patients through the full spectrum of reproductive health, preventing pregnancy, managing complications, and preserving choice. In that moment, I had a choice, and I chose to continue. To be honest, I can't say what I would have done under different circumstances. If I had been told that continuing the pregnancy would leave me unable to have another, perhaps my decision would have been different. Life is not black and white. I wish more people could see and understand that.

A few weeks before James was born, my colleagues at Lewisville Family Practice threw a baby shower for me. It was a touching moment, filled with tears of joy and sadness alike. From the moment I learned of James' diagnosis, I had shared the news with them. Though I hadn't been at the practice long, I had developed a close bond with my colleagues. Family physicians are at the heart of medicine, and their extended love and support meant the world to me every day. I continued working until I was 35 weeks pregnant, but due to complications, James had to be born at 36 weeks.

My patients were unaware of the challenges we faced; all they knew was that I was expecting a baby boy. One patient even made a baby blanket for me, a sweet gesture that touched my heart deeply. She was overjoyed for us, thrilled that my husband would finally have his son. I couldn't bear to tell her that James was not expected to survive. As my pregnancy progressed, my growing abdomen became more noticeable, inviting comments and congratulations from patients. With each well-meaning remark, it became increasingly difficult to hold back tears during visits. In those moments, my colleagues were my pillars of strength, offering unwavering support and understanding when I needed it most. Their love sustained me, and I am forever grateful to them.

James taught me powerful lessons about the masks we wear. I began to look at strangers differently, wondering about their hidden struggles. Years later, rounding at the hospital, I would watch people step off elevators, their faces carefully composed yet betraying profound pain to those who knew how to look. I saw how masterfully we hide our suffering, how alone we choose to be in our grief.

My elderly patients especially moved me. In my thirties, their decades of accumulated losses humbled me, adult children taken too soon, loved ones lost to wars and disasters, dreams surrendered to time. Each wrinkle seemed to tell a story of rooted strength, of shoulders that had carried unimaginable burdens. I wondered why we as a human race had learned to hide these stories, to isolate ourselves behind carefully constructed facades.

When I saw a friend with terminal cancer watching his children play, I recognized that look in his eyes, the knowledge that he wouldn't see their graduations, their weddings, their children. No one else noticed, but I understood. James had taught me to see the fragility of life, to recognize that behind every face might lie a story of profound joy or devastating loss. If only we could lower these masks, share our vulnerabilities, perhaps we could better support each other through life's inevitable sorrows. We are all suffering in some way, but we suffer alone by choice, by custom, by fear.

***

We brought James home exactly 18 hours after his birth. After my third C-section, the nurses assured me my Foley catheter would be removed by 11 PM. When that time came and went without anyone appearing, I took matters into my own hands, asking my husband to find a 10cc syringe so I could remove it myself. By midnight, a nurse finally arrived, but I informed her I had already taken care of it and had even managed to void successfully. Concerned about my well-being due to significant blood loss, the attentive nurses kept checking in on me throughout the night, disrupting my attempts to rest.

When my doctor finally arrived, I insisted it was time to go home. Perhaps she understood, especially knowing I had both my mother and mother-in-law, retired nurses, as well as my husband, a pulmonary critical care physician, ready to care for me at home. Being a patient felt confining, almost like being in prison – wearing their clothes, eating their food, following their schedule. As I was wheeled out of the hospital, I breathed a sigh of relief, feeling liberated.

Reflecting now, I realize my behavior might have seemed dramatic, but the truth is doctors and nurses often struggle as patients themselves. We all know it, we joke about it, but we can't seem to do anything about it. Part of the issue lies in our medical system. They put people who have no business being in the business of people in charge. They put people with only business experience in charge of lives, and sometimes they put doctors who don't know how to run a business in charge of running one. I don't understand why doctors don't receive leadership and business education in medical school.

    I trusted my doctor, I trusted the nurses, but I didn't trust the system. I still don't trust the system. A system that tries to tell me what test to run, how long I need to see my patient, and sets my limitations. Insurance companies and hospitals setting prices, run by people who base everything on numbers. Ultimately, that is what patients are to them, a number. And no, I will not be a number. And no, the people that I love and the patients that I care for will not be a number. Humanity is too valuable, too precious for the system.

    Medicine is incredible, and we have come a long way, heading towards places we can only imagine. We can't let, I can't allow the system to control me, to tell me how to doctor, how to treat people like human beings. I guess this is why, as a healthcare provider, I don't like to be a patient. I just know too much.

    I was tired, and I knew my time would be limited with my son. I needed to take in every day, every hour, every minute, every second. Smell his baby smell, show him the world, or at least as much of it as I could before he died. I needed to nurse my baby, rock him to sleep, take him on walks, to the park. I had to fit a lifetime of experiences into the time I had left. I had no idea how much time I had, but I was going to make every moment count. He was going to live, he was going to live, and he was going to live some more.

We often forget how time passes us by. We squander the day, we don't call the people we love, thinking we'll call them the next day. But the next day could mean that person is no longer here to talk to. How careless we are with the time we're given, never really knowing how much that is. How careless we are with forgetting to spend time with the ones we love. How careless we are when it comes to picking up the phone and talking to a loved one. The hours pass, and we don't think about it until someone tells us our time is limited. Our life is limited. This was the valuable lesson I learned from my patients: make every second count.

The amazing thing is that as soon as I forget this lesson, another patient teaches me again and again. We shouldn't wait until we're on our deathbed for our children to come and say goodbye; we should spend time with them when we're able to actually be present. I was going to be present. My patients taught me that.

***

Love has always surrounded me and covered me like a coat in a cold storm. My entire pregnancy was filled with tears. Every time I went in for an ultrasound or to discuss what was going on, I cried. But people surrounded me and protected me. I often cried into my husband's chest, sobbing, unable to breathe, and he just held me. He held me until I had no more tears. My mother, my mother-in-law, my father, my father-in-law, my sister, my sister-in-law, my aunt, my uncle, cousins, friends, co-workers, my children, and my church surrounded me and protected me.

They all had a role to play, and I came to understand what love and support truly meant.

I look at pictures from those days, and I see how I was in denial. I started to forget that my son was sick. He looked so normal, he seemed to be growing and thriving. But the pictures tell a different story. They show a mother in denial, a blue baby because he didn't have enough oxygen circulating in his little body, and a family holding on to each other.

Looking back at those pictures, I realize I was a bit selfish. I yelled at my mother and mother-in-law, who were always there for me. I told them they didn't understand what I was going through. But they did understand, and perhaps they were enduring even more than I was. They were watching their daughter and son lose a child, and they were witnessing their grandchild die. These two mothers were at the heart of it all, and despite my anger and harsh words, they remained steadfast by my side. Both of these women were nurses; they had seen pain and death in both their personal and professional lives. I know that now, and I see that now.

***

When James was three days old, we took him to the park. I watched as Jas held him, brushing his tiny feet against the grass and then the sand. James seemed to love the feel of the sand against his baby feet. I saw Jas ride down a slide with him, and behind my sunglasses, I started to cry. Tears ran down my cheeks as I tried to hold them back; I didn't want my mother and father to see my pain. I could see they were hurting too.

Watching my husband with his son, I cursed God under my breath, questioning why He was teasing us, why He planned to take our son away. This might have been the last time James would slide down a slide or feel the sand or grass beneath his feet.

Born in early spring, James got to see the Easter Bunny. At a full 4 lb 6 oz, we took him on a hayride. We included him in all our family outings; we even went to a bar with his cousin Ari so the boys could have that experience. James wouldn't get to grow up and play sports, go to college, talk to his cousin on the phone, or go out together and pick up girls. So my baby went to the bar for lunch when he was three weeks old. We took him to restaurants, shops, and festivals. During March Madness, James watched basketball with his father, the two lying on the floor in front of the TV, Jas holding his little hand.

Through all this, the hospice nurse would visit. I didn't really understand why because my child was healthy. Or at least I thought he was healthy. The cardiologist had surely made a mistake, a big mistake. They had lied to me, and there was nothing wrong with him. I told my husband that we had been lied to and we needed to get another echocardiogram (an ultrasound of the heart) to show that his heart was perfectly normal.

Unfortunately, I was wrong, and his heart was really broken. He still had a severe form of heterotaxy, and he was dying. One day when the hospice nurse visited, James stared at her for a long time, it was almost like they were communicating. She said he was so wise, I had not looked at him that way. I looked into his eyes, and I could see that there was so much more to them than I had noticed. He was in fact wise; it was almost like he knew his time was limited. I held my baby tighter, I cried more and didn't understand what was going on. My mother came to stay with us about two weeks before James was born to provide support and she stayed until he passed.

One day we were sitting in the living room, and my mentor Dr. Skully called me on my cell phone. He said, "Gol can I come visit you?" and I said "sure, please come visit, anytime you like", he had heard of what was going on with me and drove down and stopped by at my home in Winston-Salem to see me. It meant so much to me to see him.

As my program director during my Geriatric Fellowship, Dr. Skully would often challenge my thinking process as a doctor, always pushing me to see beyond the obvious. He didn't just teach medicine; he showed us how to be complete physicians, spouses, and parents through his own example. When I was scared of performing a procedure, he would boost my confidence, reminding us that as geriatricians, we could only offer to make things a little better, the situation was already difficult enough. Now, holding James, I understood how those lessons would help me care for my own son.

I understood this even more deeply a few years later when I became a program director myself. My old fellows became like family, just as my mentors had been for me. These connections, these lessons passed down through generations of physicians, created a foundation of knowledge and compassion that sustained me through James's life and beyond. Dr. Skully's annual Christmas letters remain a reminder of this continuity, this passing of wisdom from teacher to student to patient, and beyond.

Each of my mentors had given me a piece of what I would later need.

Dr. Herzog taught me how to stay composed when the ground beneath me felt uncertain, a skill that held me together during James's final weeks.

Dr. Holt taught me to explore every possibility, to ask every question, which became essential as I tried to understand James's condition.

Dr. Sams taught me the balance between being a doctor and a mother, advice that took on new weight when I had to be both at once.

Dr. Marques taught me how to stay steady during crisis—lessons I drew on every single day.

And Dr. Fitch and Dr. Johnson taught me the value of slowing down and being fully present, the patience I needed to care for James moment to moment.

    Dr. Skully held James and commented that he was like an old person. Intrigued, I looked at James and realized the truth in his words. I had seen this before, particularly with patients who couldn't express themselves, those with severe dementia or those nearing the end of life. I treated these patients by sensing their needs. When a person with dementia screams or gets aggressive, it could indicate pain or fear. When a dying patient starts to grimace, their muscles tighten, and their respiratory rate increases, it may be a sign of pain. In a way, my experiences had trained me to care for my dying son, to be attuned to his actions and try to figure out if he was hungry, in pain, or short of breath. As always, I appreciated Dr. Skully's insight and teachings, knowing this advice would be invaluable in the weeks to come.

    A few weeks went by, and at seven weeks old, I noticed a change in James. He wasn't eating as much, seemed more agitated, and appeared short of breath. I remember Jas telling me it was time to give him some oxygen, perhaps morphine and lorazepam. It was incredibly hard for me to put my baby on oxygen and to give him those medications. When I administered morphine, his breathing would slow, he could sleep, but he wouldn't eat, and I constantly questioned if I was doing the right thing. Sometimes, I hesitated to give him the medications, causing us to fall behind on his comfort and then struggle to catch up. Looking back, I realize I was prolonging his suffering and his death. As I write these words, I am reminded of another mentor, Dr. Gordon, who wrote a book called *A Death Prolonged*. Dr. Gordon was a cardiologist who understood life and death profoundly, shaped by the changes in medicine and the hospital environment. I always enjoyed discussing his perspectives.

The next lesson I learned from my patients was understanding when enough is enough and recognizing the importance of quality of life. Jas also came to this realization. By the time James was born, Jas was nearly finished with his medical training. He had completed three years of Internal Medicine, two years of Pulmonary Medicine fellowship, and was well into his Critical Care training, set to finish within three months. I had been working for three years as an attending physician after completing three years of Family Medicine residency and one year of Geriatrics fellowship. Before medical school, I earned a Master of Science in Gerontology, which taught me the psychosocial aspects and needs of the aging population.

When we found out early on about James's heterotaxy diagnosis, we learned how difficult his life would be, and we did not want our son to suffer. In our medical training, we often faced situations where we watched people suffer because their family members couldn't let go. They kept them on ventilators for far too long, insisted on tube feedings, and prolonged their suffering until their loved ones died in pain. Conversely, we also witnessed family members who advocated for peace and comfort, recognizing when enough was enough and allowing their loved ones to pass with dignity.

I wanted James to die with dignity. I wanted him to experience life in a meaningful way, and I believe we gave him just that, and he gave us so much more in return. The day before he died, my husband and I looked at him, and Jas said, "I think he is ready to go." James seemed deep in thought, his little eyes wandering around the room, his blue face with the oxygen nasal cannula on. We held him, kissed him, and tried to keep him as comfortable as possible. There was an indescribable calm in our home that day.

Mila and Zoey came home from daycare, we played, I watched our little boy, knowing this was the last day he would be with us. Jas and I kept exchanging glances, checking on each other, watching and waiting. Every couple of hours James would start to cry, he would grimace, he would start breathing heavier, faster, deeper. This is when we knew he was struggling, we knew we needed to give him a little morphine, to help him relax into his breathing. Even though I had learned my lesson from falling behind on his comfort by delaying on the morphine, it still bothered me to administer it.

We went to sleep that night, and around two AM, we woke up to him breathing rapidly and appearing uncomfortable. We gave him one dose of morphine to calm his breathing, and he was at peace again. I watched my little boy, held him, and told him it was okay to go home. I told him that I would miss him, but I didn't want him to suffer. I had learned this from the loving hospice nurses I had worked with in the past. I had learned that sometimes loved ones need our permission to let go, that they hold on as long as they can, struggling because they worry about us, the ones who remain. So just like I had learned, just like I had repeated those words to patients and their loved ones, I myself whispered those words, "go home baby, it's okay, we will be ok, we will miss you, go home". He took a deep breath in, a deep breath out, and passed.

Jas was lying next to us, dozing in and out of sleep, waking up every 5-10 minutes to see if we were ok. I tapped him on his shoulder and told him that James was gone. Although expected, he had a surprised expression on his face. Time slowed as I held James, Jas held James, sitting in the dark on our bed staring in silence. James was gone.

I don't remember exactly when I called hospice, but the hospice nurse arrived about 30 minutes later. She was so kind; hospice nurses are a special breed of human. Their warmth and kindness have no bounds; they give and give. I often wonder if they have enough for themselves. She instructed us to call the funeral home when we were ready. So I just held James for another few hours. His skin began to cool, the color faded, and he appeared white, his lips were blue, and his little body started to go rigid. I wasn't ready to let go, and despite these changes I held onto his cool rigid body, knowing it was for the last time. When our little girls woke up, they held James and kissed him goodbye. The funeral home came and took him away.

Three days later, they returned with a box of his ashes. The silence of his death was deafening. I felt empty, defeated, angry, and sad. I was so many things, but more than anything, I was a mother who had lost her son.

After James's death, my sister Golnar reminded me of something profound. Since I had left Salt Lake City for medical school, my sister had moved to the East Coast. We were always close, but life had scattered us. James brought us all together during this incredible time; that little baby bound us to each other again. His existence brought us closer than we had ever been, helping me see the warmth and love that family provides and why it is so important to hold on and not let small things get in the way.

Reflecting on this, I realized how fortunate I was, especially considering some of my patients who had been estranged from their sisters, brothers, or children. I was thankful that James tightened our bond. No matter how angry we get at each other in this family, the next day seems to be just fine. We pick up from a place of love and care for each other.

Through work with patients, a profound lesson has been learned about the regret that comes from cutting ties with family and loved ones over trivial matters. These were often small unimportant issues that, over time, grew to create a deep chasm between them. For some, it is parents estranged from their adult children; for others, it is adult siblings consumed by anger and stress. In all cases, it is a tragic waste of precious, limited time that could have been spent together.

As my parents have aged, we've realized the importance of being close to each other. Although we were once scattered across the country, we now live within minutes of each other. I've learned that through the most difficult times in our lives, we will always be there for each other, without judgment or anger. That is what matters most. We are fragile, but we are stronger when we are bound.

I used to watch adult children with their aging parents, seeing how these parents supported them and stayed by their side as they were dying, talking to them, loving them, thanking them for everything. I wanted that for James, and I want that for our family. The love and support we give each other through all the hardships make life meaningful and bearable.

Life is beautiful, and this adventure cannot be experienced alone.

Chapter 2

The Power of Love

Love is the eternal whisper that shapes our existence; it is the heartbeat of the soul. What is life's purpose if love does not grace our journey? How can we savor joy, mourn sorrow, embrace hope, or understand despair without love's touch?

I could not write this book without acknowledging Alma Richards. Alma was my closest friend for a significant part of my childhood. When we moved to Salt Lake City, I was about 9 years old. My parents, apprehensive about living in a house, settled us into a two-bedroom condominium. Down the hall lived an elderly lady named Alma. Alma was a pivotal figure in my growth. A widow who had spent much of her youth traveling with her father in the military, she had lived in the Philippines and China. Her round face puzzled me at the time, but I later understood when I was in medical school that it was likely due to steroid treatment for her lung disease. Despite being in her early 80s, she had remarkably smooth skin for her age, something she attributed to an incident in childhood. Alma shared with me that, at around 6 years old, she had spent too long in the cold in China, and her face froze. Although I never fully grasped it, she believed this was why she remained relatively wrinkle free.

Alma was mostly confined to her apartment with her two cats. She suffered from emphysema, though not due to smoking; she had never smoked. Alma recounted a night when she had fallen asleep in her husband's office, which had just been painted. The fumes from the paint caused her severe illness, leading to hospitalization and chronic progressive lung disease. Her husband, Bert, was her third fiancé. Her first two suitors died during World War II; one of them perished in the war while she was living in Germany. She recalled how challenging it was to live in Germany during the World War II. Although she was technically safe as an American, she was stranded and unable to return to the States. When Alma shared stories from her past, her eyes would transform, as if she were reliving those moments. Some stories were filled with beauty and joy, often from her childhood or from her time with Bert. Others were tinged with sadness, reflecting her experiences during the war.

Despite her own suffering, Alma's love for life was profound. One winter, she discovered a katydid on her porch and tenderly cared for it throughout the season. Her dedication ensured that the katydid survived until spring, even though its natural lifespan was only about a year. Alma's compassion extended beyond animals to everyone she encountered. My grandfather, who spoke no English, would sit beside her and watch television with her, drawing comfort from her silent companionship. The strength Alma provided was palpable; she supported not only my sister and mother but the entire neighborhood. Her presence, despite her frailty, was a source of emotional sustenance for all of us. One of my fondest memories is of sitting with her, watching "Dr. Zhivago," a simple yet cherished moment that encapsulated her nurturing spirit and the depth of her care.

Alma had a dear friend whose young daughter she cherished. They often spent time together, and Alma spoke of the little girl with warmth and affection. One night, as the bombings grew dangerously close, Alma sensed something was terribly wrong. The next day, she learned that her friend and the child had been killed when their apartment building was struck. War had a way of stealing relationships overnight, some friendships faded with distance; others were taken by violence. Food was scarce, water was often unavailable, and she sometimes bathed using only a small bowl. Though she survived, Alma carried a quiet guilt, never fully understanding why those she loved were gone while she remained.

As I grew older, I watched Alma change, her strength softening into frailty. She was a refuge for my sister and me, her door always open, her presence steady and reassuring. In contrast, my father's world felt heavy and storm-torn. Before the revolution, he had been a respected civil engineer in Iran —

successful, confident, and surrounded by the life he had built. But everything he knew was uprooted. He lost his work, his community, and a sense of identity he had spent years shaping. In Salt Lake City, he felt invisible and undervalued, a newcomer in a place that could not see the life he had once lived. His frustration grew as opportunities shrank, and as a child, I mistook his grief for anger. I didn't yet understand the depth of his loss; I only sensed a distance where I had once felt closeness.

My parents' move to the United States was a profound act of love, not a simple change of address. They left behind privilege, careers, and community to give us a chance at something better. Growing up in Salt Lake City, I often felt like an outsider — dark hair and eyes in a culture where I visibly stood apart. We had little compared to other families, and I learned to think like an adult early on. Perhaps that perspective is what led to my unexpected friendship with an eighty-year-old woman, a relationship that shaped the way I saw aging, tenderness, and resilience. Looking back, I am profoundly grateful for the path my parents chose. Their sacrifices, Alma's stories, and the contradictions of my childhood all led me to the life I live today.

As an adult, I have come to understand that children perceive the world in much simpler terms, good and bad, without the complexities that adults navigate. We can shape our children's lives profoundly, either building them up or breaking them down. I often reflect on how my own words and actions might impact my children and feel a pang of guilt. Yet, I am reminded of my father, who, despite his struggles and frustrations, is fundamentally a kind and loving man. Becoming adults ourselves allows us to love our parents in a different way, recognizing that they too had to navigate through hardship, it helps us to see more clearly. Even more so, becoming a parent helped me to grasp how difficult it was for my parents to raise children. Shit, under my care two of my children have had broken bones, and all at some point have needed stitches, yet my sister and I as children never had a broken bone or a stitch under my mothers care.

Alma helped me see the sacrifices my parents made and reminded me that their love for me was steadfast. Through her wisdom, I learned that the adult world is intricate and that what I perceived as flaws or failings in my parents was not the full picture. Now, as I replay her words in my mind, I recognize how much they helped me understand my father's efforts and the depth of his love, even in the midst of his personal turmoil.

When Bert and Alma met, her belief in love was rekindled. After enduring the loss of friends, family, and lovers she had hope again. Bert, the man who discovered ozone in the atmosphere, brought a new dawn into her life. Their marriage, though childless, was filled with deep affection and companionship. Bert was older, and their love was a testament to enduring commitment and joy. Though Bert's passing left Alma heartbroken, she cherished the opportunity to love once more. She often shared with me that the love between a man and a woman is something one must experience firsthand to truly understand. I think of her words often, especially when reflecting on my own relationship with my husband.

In my practice, I see a reflection of this profound love in the lives of my patients, Terri and Will. They have been married for decades, and their mutual support is extraordinary. They function as a single unit, with each one feeling the other's pain and joy as their own. Their bond is so intertwined that when one is affected by pain or illness, the other shares in the experience. Their unwavering love and advocacy for each other are evident in every gesture and look. Will's gaze at Terri is reminiscent of a teenager's first love, bright, eager, and filled with admiration. Yet, this youthful excitement is underscored by a lifetime of shared experiences, making their love as profound and enduring as anything I've ever witnessed.

***

When love walked into my life, it happened in the most unexpected way. I was visiting an old attending physician, Dr. Reese, may he rest in peace, at Kings County Hospital in Brooklyn, when I first met my husband. Sitting in a small conference room, I noticed a tall, skinny, blonde, blue-eyed young man walk in and take a seat. His confidence and charming smile immediately caught my attention. I was discussing a silly mistake I had made on a test with Dr. Reese when Jas, as he later introduced himself, interrupted with a straightforward correction. His assertiveness and clarity struck me deeply. Although he was only in the room briefly, I was drawn to him in a way I couldn't ignore. As soon as he left, I asked Dr. Reese to tell me everything about him. Dr. Reese spoke highly of Jas, praising his exceptional work ethic and no-nonsense attitude. He suggested I join the group of medical students for dinner that night to celebrate the end of their rotation.

The twelve-week medicine rotation at Kings County Hospital was grueling, on call every third night, working 15-18 hours a day, and perpetually exhausted. We were always hungry, always worried about making mistakes, and afraid of the attending's reprimands. Yet, amidst the chaos, meeting Jas felt like a beacon of hope. Despite only dating for about three months, one of which was spent in Salt Lake City helping my mother recover from knee surgery, I was infatuated with him. When he proposed, I was surprised, but there was something irresistible about him, a closeness I hadn't felt with anyone else. We shared deep insights and an understanding that made our connection profound. Jas is someone you either love or don't like at all, he's brutally honest and straightforward. I appreciate this quality deeply; I don't like ambiguity or beating around the bush. I want clear, honest answers, and Jas provides exactly that.

My time at Kings County Hospital taught me that patients always come first, before family, sleep, mental health, food, and even a simple breath. I practically lived at the hospital during that period. The old hospital building had been converted into dorm rooms for students, offering cheap rent compared to local apartments. My room was a cramped four-by-six space, furnished with a worn hospital bed and a dresser. The bathroom and showers were down the hall, and the building, likely over a hundred years old, exuded a musty smell with dark, shadowy corridors. Often, I was so frightened of the dark hallways at night that I would hold off using the bathroom until absolutely necessary.

My days began at 4 AM, ensuring I could be at the hospital by 5 to pre-round on my patients. The expectation was to review each patient's condition, including the last 24 hours' events, lab work, consults, and imaging. By 9 AM, when our attending physician arrived for rounds, we had to be prepared to present each case. Each attending had their own approach, but Dr. Reese, a larger man, preferred to sit in the conference room first and review cases before rounding with us. He was notorious for his probing questions, designed to test our medical knowledge. While standing by the patient's bedside, his questions would continue, and I would feel a rising panic. My heart would race, my palms would sweat, and I braced myself for the possibility of his reprimands. Despite my fears, Dr. Reese was notably less harsh with me than with some of the other students. His criticism, though firm, was tempered with patience and a semblance of kindness, providing a small solace amid the intense pressure.

Around the second week of my rotation at Kings County Hospital, I found myself alone in the conference room, immersed in studying and catching up on progress notes. Dr. Reese walked in and took his usual place at the head of the table. With only the two of us in the room, my nerves were on edge. I muttered a hesitant "Good morning" and kept my head down, dreading any further interaction.

As minutes ticked by and my heartbeat gradually slowed, I hoped that this would be a quiet encounter. But then Dr. Reese turned to me and asked why I wanted to become a doctor and what my future plans were. In that moment, my fear momentarily receded as I spoke about my passion for aging, a passion shaped by caring for my grandfather as he aged and passed away, and by completing a master's degree in Gerontology. I explained that my goal was to help people and that becoming a Geriatrician was my path to making the most impact.

For the first time, I felt a wave of confidence as I shared my aspirations. Dr. Reese listened intently and then surprised me with a warm smile. He revealed that he was living with and caring for his own mother and admitted he had never had a student express a desire to specialize in geriatrics. His admiration was evident as he told me, "You will never do anything wrong in my eyes again!" So if any medical students happen to read this book, consider Geriatrics, it's the best, the most rewarding profession in medicine. Not only will your life be more enriched by the lessons you learn from your patients, you may also have a more enjoyable experience as a student.

This pivotal moment shifted our relationship from one of fear to mentorship. Dr. Reese's questions became less threatening and more instructive. He guided me through challenges without the harshness I had feared, and I found myself thriving under his mentorship. It was the love of medicine, the love of healing the wounded, and the wisdom I would gain from my patients that kept me going. I was genuinely happy during that rotation, eager to tackle 24-hour shifts, rise at 4 AM, and collapse into my tiny, dark dorm room by evening. Though the rotation remained demanding, the supportive dynamic with Dr. Reese made all the difference.

When I completed my 12-week rotation, I eagerly requested to return for a 4-week elective, much to the bewilderment of my fellow students who thought I was insane. But I had found a home at Kings County Hospital, so much so that I even stayed on for a psychiatry rotation. Dr. Reese and I continued our friendship beyond my rotation. He was aware of my life in New York, including the less-than-ideal relationships I had been navigating, especially one particular toxic individual who barely merits mention.

One Thanksgiving, after an emergency room shift, Dr. Reese made sure I wasn't alone by taking me out to dinner. This gesture of kindness was just one of many that deepened our bond. Every 2-3 months, I would take a train to the hospital, bringing lunch and catching up with him in the conference room. It was during one of these visits that I saw Jas in the same conference room, seated in the same chair where I had sat a year earlier. It was a moment of serendipity that intertwined my past and present, revealing how far I had come and how interconnected our lives can become.

That evening, Dr. Reese picked me up from my Brooklyn apartment, and we went to dinner with the rest of the medical students. At the time, I was a fourth-year medical student, while Jas was in his third year. After dinner, the group planned to continue their evening in the city for drinks and invited me to join them. Dr. Reese, with a serious tone, looked at Jas and said, "James, I expect you to get her home safely; she's like family to me." And so, with that reassurance, Jas and I ventured into the city together.

Although we went as a group, Jas and I found ourselves separated from the crowd and ended up at a bar somewhere in the Lower East Side. The bar, with its shag carpet and black and white checkered tiles, felt like a scene straight out of an Austin Powers movie. As we realized the rest of the group was nowhere to be found, it didn't matter; I wanted to be near him, just him and his smile. We eventually left the bar to rejoin the others, who had moved to a different place. As we waited at the corner of a busy New York City street, he looked down at me, and in that moment, we shared a kiss.

Although I didn't see him for about a week afterward, when we finally met again at his home, we spent nearly every day exploring the city together. I fell deeply and profoundly into his blue eyes, butterflies and all. Alma was right, she was always right.

The love between a man and a woman is something so unique, it cannot be truly explained. Even now, years later, I still feel that same infatuation. I get so excited when he comes home, and we've developed an understanding of each other's expressions. He knows mine as well as I know his. His hair has started to gray at the sides, and wrinkles have gathered around his eyes. We both have entered the realm of middle age, but when I look at him, I still see that young man from our first meeting. The essence of who he was back then, his charm, the warmth, and the deep connection, remains unchanged, and he continues to change the direction of my life.

Another invaluable lesson I learned from Alma, as well as from observing my parents' tumultuous relationship, was the importance of avoiding unnecessary drama. Having experienced relationships filled with upheaval and emotional turbulence, I knew I wanted something different. Jas, with his steady and composed demeanor, was the antithesis of drama. Even now, when my Persian blood boils with stress, he senses my anxiety and calmly says, "Hakuna Matata." And he's always right, those things that seem so significant in the moment are often just trivial concerns. His calm presence and unwavering support remind me of what truly matters and help me keep things in perspective, making our life together one of love, peace and understanding.

By the time I was 28 and had met Jas, I knew I needed a partner who would challenge me, someone who, like me, was driven to grow and strive for more. Jas embodied that spirit. While we are content with what we have, we both recognize that there is always room for growth. I have learned that I can always be a better mother, daughter, sister, and wife. I constantly strive to improve as a doctor and a businesswoman, embracing the lessons life teaches me each day. Our mutual desire to learn, to better ourselves, and to support each other is our greatest asset. Jas is consistently there for me, often more than I can say I am for him. He fiercely protects our family and my heart. As I watch him evolve over the years, his unwavering devotion to us remains a constant source of strength and reassurance.

When our son James was dying, I remember countless moments when I buried my head in Jas's chest, sobbing uncontrollably as he held me tight. Despite the devastating reality that his own son was slipping away, Jas was my rock, unwavering and strong. He provided me with comfort and strength, embodying a love that transcended the unbearable grief we both faced. It wasn't until years later, as I started to process the loss without being overwhelmed by tears, that I realized my own shortcoming. I was so consumed by my own sorrow that I wasn't fully present for Jas. The guilt I feel is a testament to the realization that we were not just enduring the death of our son alone; we were navigating this profound loss together. Jas didn't seek support from others; he stood steadfast for us, his family, protecting us while no one was there to protect him. His strength and love during that time taught me that love isn't just about being there for each other in moments of happiness but also about sharing the weight of the deepest sorrows.

So embrace love, love and be loved.

Chapter 3

The In Between: Making Moments Matter

From the moment we enter the world until our last breath, we navigate the spaces in between. It's within these moments that we learn to crawl, walk, and run; we discover what it means to be, to love, and to overcome. While we may strive for grand achievements, the true significance often lies in the simple, everyday experiences. Cherishing these in-between moments, holding onto the beauty of life as it unfolds, gives our journey meaning and depth. As our petals wilt and we retreat to rest before life's end, we reflect on what matters most—those cherished moments that define our existence.

When I reflect on the theme of life, love, and the spaces in between, I think deeply about what it truly means to be alive. It's a journey marked by a spectrum of experiences, the joy and sorrow, the moments within and beyond our control. Through it all, love finds us, and the in-between moments, whether they lift us to new heights or bring us to our knees, are what sustain us. As someone deeply immersed in the business of the human experience, I can't help but grapple with these themes daily. My work compels me to confront the meaning of life regularly, and while this constant reflection can be daunting and might seem overly philosophical to some, I consider it a profound gift.

Becoming a physician, I never anticipated that this role would lead me to such profound introspection. Yet, as fate would have it, this profession has given me something invaluable. It's not just about healing my patients; it's about how my patients, in turn, help me see the bigger picture. Even in my most intense struggles, those moments when I felt I was losing my grip entirely, this gift of reflection has been a grounding force. Though some might argue that I haven't always been as grounded as I could be, knowing myself, I realize that without this reflective practice, I might have fallen much further.

In a culture that often sets aside its elders and views aging negatively, despite it being a universal journey, I feel a deep responsibility to share the wisdom of the elders I have had the privilege of treating. Their experiences and insights are often overlooked, but they hold valuable lessons that can profoundly enrich our understanding of life. This perspective not only helps me remain anchored but also inspires me to honor and amplify the voices of those who have lived through the very realities we all face.

I remember a moment when my daughter Mila, at just twelve years old, asked me a question that took me by surprise: "What is the point?" We were discussing school and my educational journey, college, graduate school, medical school, and more, and she wanted to understand why all of it mattered in the face of our mortality. Her question initially felt heavy and unsettling, making me wonder if she was struggling with hope or dreams.

As our conversation continued, I realized Mila's question wasn't born from despair but from a genuine curiosity about life and death. I explained to her the marvel of the human brain and how, through our knowledge and innovations, roads, cars, hospitals, airports, and humans have created a world unlike any other species. Growth, I told her, comes from learning and passing on that knowledge to future generations, always holding onto hope that life will continue to improve, that life will go on even after we're gone. Our responsibility is not just to ourselves, but our future generations.

Mila's response, her excitement about going to college one day, reassured me that she wasn't in despair but was seeking understanding. Still, I couldn't help but wonder what prompted such a profound question from her. How could I model love, hope, and resilience for her? How could I show her that despite setbacks, failures, and tragedies, it's possible to keep moving forward?

Pema Chödrön's teachings resonate deeply with me, particularly her perspective on failure and perseverance. Her life story is a testament to the transformative power of embracing struggle. Pema Chödrön, who became a Buddhist nun in her mid-30s, faced numerous personal challenges before her spiritual awakening. Her journey wasn't easy. She navigated a difficult marriage, personal upheavals, and the complexities of raising children. Despite these trials, she found profound wisdom and peace in the face of adversity.

Her life underscores a powerful truth: that growth and steadfastness often arise from the most trying experiences. Pema Chödrön's encouragement to "fail, fail again, fail better" is rooted in her own path of overcoming difficulties and discovering strength through them. Her story exemplifies how, even in moments of struggle, we have the potential to emerge stronger and more insightful. This perspective has profoundly impacted my approach to life and patient care, reinforcing the idea that our greatest growth often comes from navigating our darkest moments.

When James died, I felt numb and immobilized. The loss was overwhelming, and I was consumed by anger and grief. I desperately wanted my child back, and I found myself questioning everything. During the time we had with him and in the moments after his passing, I struggled with feelings of betrayal and despair. His birthdays came and went without him, and the world continued to move forward, indifferent to my pain.

In my sorrow, I once wrote to God, expressing my deepest anguish and frustration. I pleaded for my child's return and expressed how, in my desperation, I would have given up everything, my faith, my beliefs, my very soul, to have him back with me. My faith in a higher power felt shattered, and I questioned how such a miracle could be taken away. I felt betrayed by the universe and struggled with anger towards everything that had once provided me solace.

The silence and void left by James's passing were deafening. My anger was directed at God, the angels, and the universe. I grappled with the enormity of the loss and the injustice I felt. It was a struggle to reconcile with a world that seemed to have taken away the purest love, my child. I told my husband that God knew I had to have Mila and Zoey first, because if James had been born first and passed, I don't think I could have gone on. But that's how life works. Even when we lose something that brings us to our knees and makes us question our existence, there is a reason to go on. My girls and my husband were my reason. They pulled me up and out of what could have been the end of me.

The in-between moments teach us about life and the importance of love. They motivate us to keep living, searching for love, and embracing each experience. The in-between is not just a phase but the essence of our journey. Unfortunately, sometimes we focus so much on what is ahead that we forget to focus on those in-between moments. I have seen this in my own life and in the lives of some of my patients.

Mary was in her 70s when we met. She was a very slender woman, always afraid of being sick. She was so afraid of living that life had passed her by. Always anxious and worried about what would happen next, she missed out on living. Any small ache, cough, or change from her baseline made her think she had a terminal illness. She would become so preoccupied with these thoughts that she couldn't focus on anything else. Her mind wandered into the future, imagining how these symptoms would lead to her death. Her constant worry made her even sicker, causing symptoms like nausea, abdominal pain, and muscle stiffness, which would lead to more negative thoughts. We often discussed these thoughts, and she would come to the realization that her worries were not rational. She understood it didn't make sense, but she couldn't move past it.

Unfortunately, Mary's story is not just her own. I have seen it repeated countless times with different patients. I often found myself wondering with my partner and colleagues: would we also become this way as we aged? Does growing older naturally bring more fear, more preoccupation with illness, more worry about the end? And if so, how heartbreaking it is to stop savoring life's moments, just when our time becomes most precious. With Mary, no reassurance could fully shift her perspective. She would often ask me directly if she was dying, or if she needed more tests, yet in the same breath would admit she did not really want the answer. As her physician, this weighed heavily on me. I feared the day when I would no longer be able to tell her that her worries were irrational, when I would have to confirm that her fear had finally aligned with reality. But in truth, all of us are moving toward that same end. Perhaps the real work is not in avoiding the thought of death, but in finding ways to gently embrace life as it unfolds, moment by moment.

Ruth was another patient troubled by her own debility and preoccupied with notions of how her medical problems would lead to her end. Our first patient visit, which lasted about three hours, took place in her home. During that time, I learned about her childhood, adulthood, her relationship with her parents, and the abuses she had endured as a child. She had been married to a man who left her, had no children, and her sister lived out of state. The trauma she endured as a child left her completely immobilized and unable to move on with her life; she was afraid of living in the moment and of the future. Although she saw a therapist routinely, the situation was not addressed when she was younger, and the internal scars and wounds of that trauma affected her entire life. She could not walk, experienced severe pain, and had heart disease, kidney disease, and other medical issues contributing to her disease burden. During most of our visits, she was tearful and afraid. There was little I could do but tend to her medical problems, sit with her, let her get her worries off her chest, and hug her. She was also preoccupied with making sure she had enough pain medication. She had been using opioids for decades, and it wasn't until about five years earlier that her pain medication regimen was reduced as physicians started to realize the dangers of opioids. Perhaps the pain management was a way to keep her numb so she didn't have to deal with her harsh past, her lonely life now, and the fear of her future.

    Ruth endured a great deal of trauma as a child, unimaginable pain that no child should ever face. In *The Body Keeps the Score*, Dr. Bessel van der Kolk explains how childhood trauma often manifests later as physical illness. When those early wounds are left unaddressed, they can shape the body and spirit for a lifetime, and true healing remains out of reach. For Ruth, the trauma had been muffled and pushed aside for decades, swept under a rug but never resolved. I often wondered whether her physical suffering might have been less severe had her emotional scars been tended to with the same urgency as her medical conditions. Instead, her days were filled with fear, preoccupation with illness, and dread of death. How can we fully live in the present when the very roots of our lives are tangled in unresolved trauma and pain? And yet, I hold hope that my generation and those that follow are more attuned to whole-body healing, seeking not just to cover wounds with bandages, but to nurture the deeper places where true restoration begins.

Mary and Ruth were paralyzed in a place where they could not find joy. How does a person end up in a state of such despair that hope seems unattainable? How can I, as a doctor, help my patients emerge from the darkness of their minds? Medical school focuses on genetics, biochemistry, anatomy, and pharmacology, leaving little room for the study of humanity. Yet, despite being immersed in the business of humanity, we rarely have the time to learn how to truly listen to and connect with our patients. It's often only in well-structured training programs or through the guidance of wise mentors that we begin to understand our own limitations as doctors and recognize the need for personal growth.

In my conversations with Ruth and Mary, I learned to simply listen, to hold space for their fears instead of prescribing answers. What they needed most was not advice, but ears. Perhaps my role was to offer comfort in those fragile in-between moments: to let them speak of their past, to name their fears, to sit beside them without judgment, to hug them, and to love them as they were. These moments of connection did not erase their pain, but they gave them a chance, however brief, to be present rather than consumed by worry. They often struggled to trust my reassurances—after all, I was decades younger, untouched yet by the depth of aging they carried. Still, I too had known trauma as a child, and perhaps that helped me understand the power of pausing with them in those in-between spaces. In the end, it was not my words but my presence that mattered most, because sometimes the smallest moments in between become the deepest form of healing.

One patient who vividly exemplified the struggle with aging and trauma was Martin. "I'm a brother, I hang with old people," Martin told me with a chuckle. Despite his self-deprecating humor, Martin and I often discussed his aging body, deteriorating memory, and the confusion these changes brought. As a Jungian psychologist, Martin had spent his life exploring the depths of the human psyche, becoming his own therapist in many ways. He applied his profound knowledge of Jungian psychology to his own experiences, trying to balance his understanding of the conscious and unconscious mind. Some of his issues were related to disease, but others were simply part of being 85 years old.

Jungian psychology, founded by Carl Jung, emphasizes the importance of the unconscious mind and its impact on our conscious experiences. Jung believed that the unconscious holds significant psychological content that influences our behaviors, thoughts, and emotions. Key concepts include the idea of the collective unconscious, archetypes, and individuation. The collective unconscious contains universal experiences shared by all humans, while archetypes are recurring symbols and themes that emerge from this shared unconscious. Individuation is the process of integrating different aspects of the self to achieve personal growth and self-awareness.

To my reader, please don't think I came to Martin with any deep knowledge of Jungian psychology, I didn't. My understanding began only after meeting him. His struggles stirred my curiosity, and I started to explore the foundations of Jung's work to see how it might shape Martin's life and, perhaps, his care. I wondered if by understanding him on that level, I could help address some of his fears. The most fascinating part of our conversations was how, when I gently reminded him of the very principles he had taught others, he would reconnect with what he believed at his core that the task of life is simply to be. And yet, even Martin forgot to live in the moment. His forgetting became a reminder for me: how easily we all drift away from presence, and how vital it is to return to those small, quiet moments in between where life is actually happening.

Despite his extensive training in Jungian concepts, Martin initially struggled to apply them to his own life. Like many healthcare providers, even psychologists, he faced the challenge of blurred boundaries between professional expertise and personal insight. It is often easier to guide others than to turn that same wisdom inward. Martin's profound knowledge did not shield him from this truth—he found it difficult to confront his own aging process and health struggles with the same clarity and compassion he had once offered to his patients.

Over time, as Martin reflected on his situation, he began to understand that he was not fully utilizing his training to address his own needs. This realization was a significant turning point. With renewed insight, Martin was able to accept his aging process and find meaning in his life despite the challenges. His reflection allowed him to embrace his condition with greater self-compassion and to see his experiences through the lens of his own teachings.

Martin had recently returned from a trip to Egypt, which he described bluntly as one he "hated." The journey had been on his wife Sarah's bucket list, so they went together. Each morning, they rose at 4 a.m. for excursions, a grueling task for an eighty-seven-year-old man. Martin felt exhausted, yet he endured it gladly, because what mattered to him was watching Sarah's joy as she finally experienced what she had always longed to see. In those moments, time seemed to slow, he watched her, he loved her, and he felt joy. Despite his own discomfort, living through her delight became his happiness. Sarah was Martin's pillar of strength, and although he rarely voiced it, his admiration for her shone through whenever he spoke her name. I did not have many conversations with Sarah myself, but through Martin I came to know her as extraordinary. She had faced her own share of challenges, including working with a group to create a home where people could die with dignity and peace. Her quiet devotion made me see her as nothing short of a saint. And it was in this story, watching Sarah's joy through Martin's eyes, that we both realized what it truly meant to live in the moment.

During our conversations, Martin frequently asked about my third child, Peyton. His genuine interest in her well-being was more than casual; he was deeply engaged in understanding how I was navigating the challenges of parenting a child with prenatal trauma. Martin admired Peyton's insightful comments and unique perspective, which shifted my own mindset. Initially, I had perceived her actions as manipulative, a common trait in young children. But Martin helped me see her as a child with a profound understanding of how to approach me, highlighting the value in every moment and the unique brilliance that can be found even in the most challenging situations.

In my practice, I often form deep connections with my patients, treating them like family. While this approach may be considered unprofessional in traditional settings, where clear boundaries are emphasized, I believe that forming such bonds is essential. Spending hours with my patients, truly getting to know them, and allowing them to know me in return enables me to advocate for them with the dedication of a family member.

A few years after becoming an attending physician, during a human resources training session, I heard a statement that changed the way I think about care: *we shouldn't want to treat someone the way we want to be treated, because what we want may not be what they want.* That truth struck me deeply, and I shifted my perspective. I realized that I needed to know my patients well enough to understand what they valued, what mattered most to them, and what they truly wanted. Only then could I advocate for them, not with assumptions, but with clarity and conviction. I became the doctor who visits patients in the hospital, tracks down hospitalists and nurses to ensure every detail is attended to, and questions them like a concerned family member. I even accompany patients to specialist appointments when I feel the notes don't fully capture their needs. My goal is to be more than just their doctor; I strive to be their sister, their daughter, and their advocate. This personal connection helps me fight fiercely for their well-being, especially in those vulnerable in-between moments where patients most need someone by their side.

Martin's struggle with aging and his insights into Peyton's situation provided me with invaluable perspectives. It underscored the importance of cherishing the in-between moments and finding meaning in everyday experiences. As I reflect on my own journey and those of my patients, I am reminded of the significance of these moments, both joyful and challenging, and of the ongoing need to grow and learn as both a doctor and a person.

To truly grasp the deep wounds our patients carry and to support their healing, we must strive to become better humans ourselves. While we may not be able to mend what is broken, we can offer comfort and solace, even if only for a moment, through our undivided attention. I found myself returning again to the lessons of Dr. Bessel van der Kolk, whose work reminded me that trauma does not simply fade with time. It lingers in the body and mind, resurfacing in ways that can keep people trapped in fear or pain.

This perspective helped me see Ruth's suffering in a new light and gave me language for what I witnessed in my daughter Peyton. Adopted as an infant, Peyton had already endured trauma before she came into our lives. Reading *The Body Keeps the Score* helped me understand that healing for her, and for so many of my patients, was not only about treating illness but about tending to hidden wounds that prevent us from living fully in the present.

In the end, making the moments matter is not about grand achievements, but about cherishing the simple, everyday experiences that shape our lives. It is in these ordinary, in-between spaces, sitting with a fearful patient, holding my child through her struggles, or sharing a quiet smile, that we discover meaning, connection, and what it truly means to live.

And yet, I still struggle every day to live in the moment, to slow down time. My impatience leaves me with guilt, as life rushes forward and expectations pull me away from what matters most. Too often I realize, only at night, that I have neglected the very things that were right in front of me. So I remind myself again and again to pause, to capture time, to create space, even if only for a brief moment. To forgive myself, and to forgive others I may hold anger or resentment toward. This is the battle we all face: the constant, necessary reminder that time is passing us by, and that our only choice is to live as fully as we can in the moments in between.

Chapter 4

The Truth Matters: How Transparency and Honesty Transform Patient Care

In the unfolding narrative of our lives, where each choice and word can shape our path, transparency is the guiding light. Honesty is not merely a principle but a promise, one that sometimes requires us to face difficult truths. Even when the truth is heavy, it is through this clarity that we navigate our path together, ensuring that we and those we care about are never misled.

In the realm of medicine, where each choice and word can shape the course of life, transparency is the light. What I say matters, and how I say things matters. In my world as a physician, my choice of words can shape and influence the decisions that my patients make. My words and actions influence how a patient or a loved one perceives me and learns to trust me. With what I do, I have to be honest. In medicine and in life, honesty is not just a principle but a promise, and sometimes, the truth requires delivering news that weighs heavily on the heart. Ensuring that the people we care for are never misled is paramount, for their lives are precious, and they deserve the clarity that truth brings.

Dan Ariely, in his book *The Honest Truth About Dishonesty*, delves into the intricacies of why people lie and how honesty can be nurtured. He reveals that dishonesty is a complex behavior influenced by personal gain, social norms, and the desire to maintain a positive self-image. Ariely's research shows that while most people wish to be honest, small lies often creep in, rationalized as harmless. I wasn't familiar with Ariely's work until much later in my career, when I decided in my early forties to pursue a master's in business with a focus on healthcare administration. At the time, I thought business school would simply make me a better physician by sharpening my leadership and management skills. What surprised me most was how much more I learned: that in business school, they actually taught about honesty, about lying, and the science behind it. Who knew? It left me wondering why medical school, a profession steeped in human trust, never touched on these lessons—how helpful it would have been to learn them earlier.

In medicine, these small lies or omissions can have significant consequences. I have seen firsthand how a lack of transparency can lead to misunderstandings, misplaced hope, or delayed diagnoses. When patients entrust their lives to me, it is my duty to honor that trust with unwavering honesty. This commitment to transparency is crucial, even when it means delivering difficult news.

However, as Ariely points out, there are times when even I am not entirely honest, despite my best intentions. One example is my patient Edward, who frequently looked for his wife, who had passed away a year earlier. At the time of her death, Edward was already suffering from moderate dementia, and his children agonized over whether to tell him. His memory reset every few minutes, and he couldn't hold onto new information. When they told him the truth, he wept bitterly. Soon he forgot why he was crying, but the sadness remained with him throughout the day. The following morning, he asked again where his wife was, and upon being told of her death once more, he grieved all over again as if hearing it for the first time. His children felt guilty and conflicted.

I advised them not to remind Edward of his wife's death repeatedly. Since he could no longer retain the memory, each reminder was a fresh tragedy. Instead, I suggested they tell him she was out, or gently redirect his focus by asking if he wanted to grab a snack while they waited for her. They could also invite him to share a story about her, allowing him to remember and cherish her in a way that brought comfort rather than pain. In Edward's case, withholding the harsh truth was an act of compassion, aimed at preserving his peace and happiness.

As I continued to see Edward and his family, they

confided how conflicted they still felt. At times, guilt led them to insist on telling him the truth, believing it was the morally right thing to do. But each time they did, he was devastated. Though his dementia quickly erased the facts, the sorrow lingered. He would cry, refuse to eat, sit in silence, and turn away from the very people trying to care for him. In those moments, the truth served the adult children more than it served Edward. It allowed them to feel they were being honest, but at his expense. Over time, they began to realize that the deeper dishonesty lay not in sparing him the painful truth, but in their own denial—denial that dementia had changed the rules, denial that their father's mind no longer worked as it once had. Facing this truth themselves freed them to understand that choosing gentleness was not deception at all, but the most loving path forward.

Ariely's insights underscore the importance of honesty not only in healthcare but in all facets of life. Whether in personal relationships, business, or everyday interactions, transparency fosters trust and respect. It allows people to face reality with clarity, enabling them to make choices that are truly in their best interest.

In my practice, I strive to embody this principle. I understand that delivering difficult news is never easy, but it is necessary. Yet I have also learned that honesty is not simply about stating the truth—it is about knowing the person at their core, understanding what they value, and listening deeply enough to speak in a way that can be received. Whether I am a physician to a patient, a daughter to a parent, or a spouse to a partner, it is this kind of honesty—rooted in compassion and understanding—that allows difficult truths to be accepted, heard, and even, at times, transformed into peace.

Just as Ariely's research illuminates the path to understanding dishonesty, our shared human experiences teach us the value of truth. It is through honesty that we build connections, navigate challenges, and find meaning in our lives. Transparency is the thread that weaves integrity into the fabric of our relationships, making them strong and enduring.

A few years ago, I was called to see a frail 70-year-old patient with pancreatic cancer to discuss goals of care. Walking down the hall to the geriatric consult, I was preparing to meet her palliative care needs. I quickly ran up the five flights of stairs, but the final ten feet to her room seemed to pass in slow motion. I had reviewed her chart with my fellow physician, John, who had told me all about her. I knew the details of her disease, the treatments she had endured, the multiple specialists involved in her care, and the results of her blood work, x-rays, and CT scans. I knew she was a "full code" patient, meaning she had chosen to receive all possible life-saving measures, including resuscitation and intensive interventions, should her heart stop or she experience severe medical complications. Despite this, I also knew that she was dying. She knew nothing about me, and although I knew so much about her, I was about to meet her for the first time.

A patient's chart is an extraordinary thing, dense with details that can make us feel as if we know a person inside and out. During a hospital admission, if the history is taken thoroughly, we learn nearly everything: each medical diagnosis they carry, their past surgeries, every medication they take, whether they ever smoked or drank, their family history, even glimpses of their social life, marriages, children, divorces, and work. We scroll through consultant notes, absorbing what the oncologist, hematologist, endocrinologist, nephrologist, or gastroenterologist has written. Each specialty adds its voice, and sometimes even conflicting opinions about treatment, opinions that may never be spoken aloud to the patient. An oncologist might quietly write that further chemotherapy is futile, while still offering a more hopeful picture in conversation. In the chart I can see imaging, the blood work, the subtle rise or fall of lab values across time, how much the patient is eating, drinking, voiding. The chart, in its sheer breadth, can be a powerful thing. It can make us believe we understand a person completely, but it is still only fragments, a record of disease and decisions, not the whole of a life.

      Looking into the eyes of the dying is a peculiar sensation. I had experienced it many times, but it never became any easier. As I looked into Carolyn's blue eyes, I knew that in a few months, she would no longer be part of this world. This feeling was common in my daily practice, though it always struck me with a deep sense of awareness. I walked into the room with my fellow physician in training, who greeted her and informed her of his return. I introduced myself as the attending physician working with Dr. Kriese. Carolyn looked nothing like the photograph in her electronic medical records, which had likely been taken several months earlier. The picture showed her with dark hair and a vibrant complexion, while now she had white, thin hair with some strands fallen out. She appeared gaunt with sunken temples, pale, and weak, with deeper wrinkles on her face. Her frailty was evident; she needed assistance to get up and use the bathroom. I thought, "Oh God, she is dying." I wondered if she could sense that I knew. Did she realize that she was nearing the end of her life?

After exchanging pleasantries, I chose to stand by the door rather than walk into the room. Just a few days earlier, I had been ill myself. I had been asked to return to work to cover the hospital during the COVID-19 pandemic, and the Centers for Disease Control had recently updated the quarantine guidelines. Two of my children had been sick with the virus, and I had developed symptoms as well. Although my COVID-19 test came back negative, I couldn't shake the worry that the test might have been inaccurate. I was only a few days out from being unwell, and under previous guidelines, I would have had to wait up to 14 days before returning to work. Now, with a more infectious strain of the virus, patients like Carolyn, with weakened immune systems, were at greater risk of severe illness and death if they contracted it. I wore my N95 mask and made sure it was sealed tightly, along with my goggles. As I walked into her room, I looked right into her eyes, and she looked back at me. There was nothing else she could truly see but my gaze.

An N95 mask is a specialized piece of personal protective equipment designed to filter out very small particles. It helps prevent the spread of the COVID-19 virus as well as other infectious agents and bacteria. As a doctor, I undergo annual fittings to ensure the mask provides a proper seal. The mask fits so snugly around my nose and mouth that it blocks out all scents. I had worn it all day and, despite my dry lips and grumbling stomach, I dared not remove it for fear of spreading illness to anyone.

The office I was given as the program director of a fellowship program was about 6x8 square feet, and I shared this space with my fellow and resident physicians. Sometimes we had a medical student, who sat on a small stool. Between the furniture and all our bodies, it was impossible for us to move our chairs at the same time and walk out of the office. As a Geriatrician, I didn't perform procedures that generated revenue for our medical center, and according to the standards and expectations of our hospital administration, I didn't see enough patients in a day. I saw sick, frail, dying patients. These patients needed my time, my compassionate care, and my ears.

I overheard a hospitalist tell a resident once that Geriatricians are "bottom feeder." To my amusement, that resident eventually became a successful and happy Geriatrician. I am thankful that she didn't listen to the advice of a burned out, unhappy physician. I am thankful that she saw the awesomeness of this specialty, because we need more Geriatrician.

"It takes a special person to do your job, to spend all that time with these patients, and I could never do that," a resident told me one day. The amusing thing was that a Geriatric colleague had shared the same story with me. He was pursuing one of those medical specialties valued by hospital administrations and didn't want to be on rotation with me. During his one-month geriatrics rotation, he showed up about half the time, was always late, made excuses for missing days, and showed no interest. A patient he saw told me he needed to listen better. I saw right through him! I have seen through people like him over the years, and honestly, I don't care what they think of Geriatrics. I love what I do. I love it because I am present; it isn't just a job or a paycheck, and what I do matters. A physician needs to understand humanity to truly care for patients. But this person, and people like him, have no business being in the business of the human connection.

I do carry my own biases when it comes to geriatrics, primary care, and even palliative care. At times, I have been critical of how these fields are undervalued or overlooked. But I must also tell you that I have encountered specialists at the very center of medicine who are extraordinary human beings, physicians who are not out of touch, but deeply present. I have known surgeons who not only do their work while their patients are under anesthesia but who follow up afterward with compassion. I have seen surgeons, cardiologists, hospitalists, oncologists, intensivists and others who bring not only skill but empathy into their practice. I think of my husband, for example, and a story once shared by a patient's family. They told me how, during a frightening time in the ICU, his calm presence and honest words gave them comfort. They felt seen, supported, and guided at a moment when they needed it most. And although the system is deeply broken, shaped by politics and hospital administrators without an ounce of empathy or patient care experience, the commitment to care still stands. These are the physicians I strive to align myself with: those who are available, approachable, and committed not just to medicine but to the people we serve. They remind me that the heart of this work is not barriers or hierarchy but love for our profession and for our patients.

Should a doctor not take on both the medical care of a patient and understand the psychosocial aspects of that person's life to better care for them? Did it not matter that Carolyn had been a nurse's aide for several years and had to move from her trailer to a friend's trailer because she could no longer afford her rent due to her cancer? Did it not matter that her children tried to exploit her financially by taking her Social Security check? Did it not matter that she lacked consistent transportation for her chemotherapy appointments? Did it not matter that she couldn't afford all her medications? Did it not matter that she experienced food insecurity? Did it not matter that she was depressed, felt hopeless, and isolated? Did it not matter that she was dying? Then what the fuck mattered? If these aspects of her life did not matter, then how could she get the treatment she needed? How could she get strong enough so the oncologist could continue treatment, and the surgeon could remove her cancer before it spread? I don't understand how the "bottom feeders" geriatricians' approach to understanding the whole patient isn't important when it comes to treating the patient?

    I've also seen this truth in my own family. My uncle was diagnosed with cancer, a disease that often takes lives far too quickly. Yet he has lived beyond the usual prognosis, and I know much of that is because of his wife, my aunt Mehranoosh. An internal medicine physician, she not only understands his medical needs but also knows how to navigate the medical system. More than that, she is a force to be reckoned with, an advocate who fights fiercely for him at every step. Watching her, I've been reminded again how much advocacy and presence matter in care, and how survival often depends on more than just medicine; it depends on someone who refuses to give up.

    I sometimes wonder if I would even be a physician today without Mehranoosh. I still remember the semester in medical school when I failed physiology. I came home devastated, hid in my mother's bedroom, and told her I wasn't going back. It was Mehranoosh who found me there, sulking, and marched upstairs. She looked me straight in the eye and said, "You're going back.

You are going to be a fantastic physician. This is just a bump in the road." She was right. My background was in behavioral sciences, and I had only completed the pre-med courses to apply to medical school. Multiple-choice tests felt impossible for me, but I could write, and I could connect. Her words lifted me off the floor and pushed me forward. Without her, I may have walked away.

Looking back now, I realize that moment was about honesty too, not the kind we practice with patients, but the kind we owe ourselves. Honesty about my limitations, honesty about my strengths, and honesty about the truth that sometimes we need someone else to see our potential more clearly than we can. Mehranoosh's unwavering belief in me helped me recognize that honesty is not only about facts; it is also about encouragement, clarity, and refusing to let fear define the story.

That lesson stayed with me years later when I met Carolyn. None of the realities of her life were in her medical chart. The chart told me about her cancer, her chemotherapy regimen, and her blood counts, but it said nothing about the life she was actually living. And yet these were the very things that determined whether she could get the treatment she needed, whether she could be strong enough for the oncologist to continue, whether the surgeon would even have the chance to remove her cancer before it spread. I don't understand how anyone can dismiss the geriatricians' so-called "bottom feeder" approach when it is precisely this whole-patient perspective that makes treatment possible in the first place.

What I knew was that between birth and death, life mattered. Amid the medical procedures, the poking, and the prodding, did we forget to tell Carolyn that she was going to die?

Did we set our expectations straight? Did we explain to her that she had a terminal illness, and regardless of what we did, our science, our technology, none of it could prevent her from dying? I knew this; I knew the cancer doctor knew this, and I knew the surgeon knew this, but did Carolyn know? When we gave her a diagnosis, did we discuss treatment options without mentioning that the treatment was palliative? Would she even have understood what that meant? Would she have grasped that palliative care meant prolonging her life while facing the inevitability of her death? Did we inform her that she would be unable to work or support herself? Did we tell her that she would lose her home? Did we, as a system, fail to explain that the treatment would make her so sick she would struggle to eat, suffer loss of appetite, fatigue, diarrhea, hair loss, numbness and tingling in her extremities, muscle atrophy, and other chemotherapy side effects? Did she know that she would be so debilitated that she might soil herself in bed while waiting for nursing staff to assist? Did we fail to acknowledge that our journey to provide medical care could strip away her dignity, her sense of self, and her identity? Did we truly disclose the cost of treatment? I didn't know because I wasn't there at the beginning. I was only called when specialists or hospitalists had exhausted their options.

Malcolm Gladwell, in his book *Talking to Strangers*, reminds us that the greatest misunderstandings often don't come from outright lies but from assumptions, assuming we understand what someone else knows, feels, or wants. In medicine, this danger is magnified. We may think a patient grasps the reality of their condition because we've explained it in clinical terms, but comprehension is not the same as understanding. With

Carolyn, I could not be sure what she truly knew. Had anyone spoken to her in plain language? Had anyone acknowledged the full weight of what she was about to endure? Gladwell's insight is a sobering reminder: honesty is not only about telling the truth but also about ensuring it is heard, received, and understood. All that remained was the truth, and it was my responsibility to help her face it with compassion.

I was called when a patient took too much of their precious, revenue-generating time, the time valued by those who ran the healthcare system. You see, what some fail to understand is that I'm not there to take; I come with hopes to replenish any sense of humanity Carolyn may have left. I thank the doctor who asked me to see her, who placed the consultation. Time slows down as I walk up the stairs, down the corridor into her room. I know what I need to do. I must help find her life, give her dignity, and provide clarity. I need to show her respect and express how much she means to me. I am a stranger who has learned about her and am now going to meet her in person. I come to help her navigate her way through her pain, her isolation, loss of self, hopelessness, depression, and anxiety to her death. You see, I cannot be a bottom feeder because there is nothing else to take from her; they have already taken everything.

I took the time to talk to Carolyn, sharing all the truths with her as compassionately as I could. I asked if she understood and if she had any questions I could answer. I inquired about her goals, fears, and thoughts. Carolyn revealed that she hadn't fully realized what her disease course would entail, and she didn't want to die in such a manner. She longed for peace, wished to avoid pain, and wanted to die on her own terms. Realizing the truth allowed her to make that decision.

It turned out that despite her frailty, Carolyn was incredibly strong. She needed to grasp the complexity of her situation. She didn't need medical jargon; she needed the truth explained to her in simple, everyday language, as if spoken by someone who wasn't a doctor. Carolyn decided to go home with hospice; she wanted to die with dignity and for the suffering to end. I did not share this with her, but I agreed with her choice. It was a decision I would have made for myself or a loved one if faced with the same fate.

What I have come to realize is that often, as physicians, we don't have all the answers. We don't always know the truth, and we must be honest about that too. Honesty is not only about naming the diagnosis or explaining the limits of treatment; it is also about admitting our own limitations. Patients don't need senseless hope, but they do need to know that we will stand beside them in uncertainty, searching for clarity together. Even when we cannot cure, even when we cannot change the outcome, we can still offer our presence, our honesty, and our commitment. Because in the end, what matters most is not having every answer, but making sure our patients know that they are not alone—that we are on their side, on their team, for as long as they need us. And the same is true for families. Honesty with a loved one does not always mean giving them the blunt truth; sometimes it means being honest with ourselves.

Edward's children eventually learned this: that sparing him the repeated tragedy of his wife's death was not deception but compassion. Their real honesty came in facing their own denial, in admitting that dementia had changed the rules. In both medicine and family, honesty is not about stripping away hope, but about choosing the kind of truth that brings dignity, peace, and love to those we care for.

If this chapter has not shown you the importance of transparency and truth, then let me give you a few more examples. As a college student, I searched endlessly for answers. You may remember I gave you a quick glimpse of my oddity as a child and middle schooler—the girl who watched *Dr. Zhivago*, wrote poetry, and had an eighty-year-old best friend. In college, I read books like Carlos Castaneda's stories of shamans seeking clarity in the mountains—silly in hindsight, yet enlightening for the eighteen- to twenty-year-old me who was still trying to understand the world. My curiosity led me to explore the words of Christians, Muslims, Buddhists, and others. I must admit that I still know little, and much of that searching stopped once I became a medical student, when all my energy was consumed by learning how to be a physician. I have never read the Bible or the Qur'an in their entirety, and my understanding of Buddhism is minuscule at best. What I do know is that my understanding of the world—and of myself—is still evolving. Perhaps that is what comes with aging: continued learning and the slow accumulation of wisdom.

What struck me, even in my limited exploration, was how each faith or philosophy placed a central value on truth. In Christianity, I found the words, *"Then you will know the truth, and the truth will set you free"* (John 8:32), and in Buddhism, I read the teaching, *"Three things cannot be long hidden: the sun, the moon, and the truth."* Of these, the Buddhist words struck me as the most beautiful, though I am not a Buddhist myself. Still, what I came to see is that while the language and teachings differ, they all point to the same essential idea: truth is not only about facts, but about freedom, justice, clarity, and compassion.

As Morrie Schwartz once said in *Tuesdays with Morrie*, *"The truth is, once you learn how to die, you learn how to live."* Carolyn, in facing the truth of her disease, found liberation in choosing dignity and peace. And Edward, through his family's recognition of what honesty truly meant, was able to live his final days with comfort rather than sorrow.

Chapter 5

Compassion in Practice: The Universal Power of Empathy

In the spaces between, compassion weaves us together. It is the soft echo of our shared humanity, where the ego dissolves and the heart's true presence shines. It is in the gentle act of letting go, in the grace of giving, and in the dance of life's infinite tenderness. With compassion as our guide, we move through existence, enveloped in love's embrace, always remembering that empathy is the essence of our being.

"Compassion is the awareness of the suffering of another and the wish to relieve it." Eckhart Tolle, *A New Earth*

Throughout the pages that follow, I share many stories — moments of tenderness, suffering, connection, and the profound lessons that patients, families, nurses, and colleagues have taught me. These examples weave together two concepts that often appear interchangeable in everyday language: empathy and compassion. But they are not the same.

Empathy is the capacity to feel with someone, to recognize their emotions and allow their experience to touch us. Compassion goes one step further. Compassion is empathy in motion: the desire not only to understand another's suffering, but to ease it, even in the smallest of ways.

This chapter highlights both qualities, sometimes subtly, sometimes overtly. My intention is not to lecture on definitions but to show, through lived experience, how empathy opens the door and compassion walks through it. The stories that follow reveal what it looks like when we allow ourselves to feel deeply and to act with intention — two forces that shape not only how we care for others, but who we become. With compassion and empathy in mind, I'd like to take you into the moments that shaped my understanding of both.

I get to know my patients deeply because I believe that true empathy stems from truly understanding them. I strive to be compassionate not merely by treating their diseases, but by treating the whole person. My approach has always been to try to go beyond medical symptoms to encompass each patient's individual needs, concerns, and life circumstances. By investing in understanding their unique experiences and challenges, I aim to offer care that is as personalized and meaningful as it is effective. This is also the space where I fall in love again and again with being a Geriatrician. This is the space that I seek when work gets hard.

This principle of compassion and understanding should extend beyond medicine into all our interactions. Whether in healthcare or our daily lives, approaching each person with empathy, seeking to understand their feelings and experiences, can transform our relationships and interactions. It's about seeing the person behind their circumstances and responding to their needs with kindness and respect. This universal application of compassion enriches all facets of life, fostering deeper connections and more meaningful interactions.

Compassion is more than feeling sympathy; it's an active response to suffering, involving both an emotional understanding of another's plight and a desire to alleviate it. This deeper form of empathy allows us to engage with others on a level that goes beyond surface interactions, promoting a more holistic approach to care and connection. Ultimately, this not only enriches the lives of those we touch but also helps us grow and find greater fulfillment in our own lives.

So here I write about empathy. It isn't written only for physicians, or even just for those who work in healthcare. Empathy belongs everywhere, in every workplace, every family, every conversation. Compassion can be practiced in the smallest of interactions, with anyone, anywhere. This book itself is about the lessons my patients have taught me. I share their stories not to focus on medicine, but because that is where I learned what it means to live, to love, and to practice empathy. Their struggles, their stories, and even their dying revealed truths that reached far beyond the clinic or the hospital.

Empathy is reciprocal. My patient, whom I will call Margaret, was dying. I thought she had weeks left. As a physician who cares for people with terminal conditions, I know we cannot say exactly when someone will die. Doctors are often wrong. The human body, the mind, and whatever lies beyond our explanation, God, the universe, have far more power than any mortal clinician. What we can do is estimate: months, weeks, days, hours. How many weeks? We really don't know. My beloved patients have surprised me many times, some hang on far longer than expected; others rally briefly, sitting up to say goodbye to a visitor or to eat a last meal they once loved. I cannot explain it.

Margaret was dying when I visited. She was sad, in pain, nauseated, barely eating and drinking. She told me she didn't know why she was still here. I told her I didn't know either. She felt lonely. Her caregiver wasn't family but a paid stranger who changed her, prepared her meals, and gave her medicines, and then retreated to the other room until Margaret needed her again. Margaret desperately wanted to be held. She had no family. She wanted to feel alive and part of the world. The pain medications meant to make her comfortable made it hard for her to use her phone to call family who lived out of town. The room felt dark; she missed sunshine. When I walked into her home, I felt that loneliness too, an overpowering, aching sadness.

My visit had been intended to be short. I came to refill medications and ensure her pain, breathlessness, and secretions were controlled. The clinical work of caring for the dying is comfort, not prolongation of life. But when the routine tasks were done, I stayed. I told her stories about my children, showed her photos from recent travels, and invited her into my life so she could connect with the world outside that room. Our visit lasted an hour and a half. I hugged her, kissed her goodbye, and promised I would return.

Later that day she messaged me, thanking me and telling me she loved me for being her doctor. What struck me was that the gratitude went both ways. I had gone there to ease her pain, yet she eased mine too. In those moments, she gave me the gift of listening, of reminding me of what mattered most. That is the essence of empathy: it does not flow in only one direction. Empathy is an exchange. I felt her suffering, and she felt my humanity. She let me in, and in return, I was able to give her life, but she gave me life back.

***

Empathy can be learned. One year, I was tasked with teaching empathy to Internal Medicine interns. Despite a growing body of evidence highlighting empathy's value in medical practice, the reception to these lessons was mixed. Some residents were highly engaged, eagerly absorbing the concepts and discussions, recognizing empathy's importance in enhancing patient care. Teaching compassion to medical interns requires more than lectures; it involves immersive experiences.

I used case studies to demonstrate empathy's impact on patient outcomes. For example, we analyzed cases where compassionate care led to improved patient satisfaction and recovery rates, showing how empathy can transform the patient experience. By encouraging interns to engage in reflective practice and active listening, they learn to integrate empathy into their daily interactions with patients. However, there were others who viewed the lessons with skepticism. Some grumbled, yawned, and rolled their eyes, clearly finding the sessions a chore. Their disinterest was palpable, and it was disheartening to see them disengaged, despite my hopes that they were at least passively absorbing the material.

This reaction made me wonder: If these individuals were reluctant to embrace empathy and compassion, why had they chosen to pursue a career in medicine? Medicine, after all, is fundamentally about understanding and caring for others. It requires a deep connection with patients, beyond the mere treatment of their illnesses. This reflection underscored the challenge of empathy training, not only in imparting skills but in aligning personal motivations with the core values of medical practice.

Reflecting on my experiences, I remember a poignant moment with a hospice nurse during James's final days. Her gaze into my small baby's eyes was a profound expression of understanding and compassion. Despite James being unable to speak, the nurse's empathy was palpable. She seemed to grasp his condition deeply, providing a level of care that transcended words.

Similarly, our palliative care provider played a crucial role during that time. I recall her soft voice as she explained what to expect, addressing each of my concerns with patience and presence. Her compassionate demeanor as I cried was a source of comfort amidst our grief. This kind of empathetic care is not just about addressing medical needs but about connecting on a deeply human level, offering solace and understanding during a time of profound loss.

These experiences reaffirmed the critical importance of empathy and compassion in healthcare. They underscore the need to see and understand patients beyond their clinical symptoms, treating them with the same depth of care and compassion that we would wish for ourselves or our loved ones. James' final days were marked by exceptional compassionate care from a hospice nurse and palliative care provider. Their actions transcended standard procedures, offering emotional support that created a peaceful and dignified environment. For instance, the nurse took time to sit with James, providing comfort and reassurance, while the palliative care provider coordinated with my family to address all our needs, both emotional and practical.

***

Robert, a man in his mid-80s, first came to my office wearing a worn red hat with a heart and the word "Jesus" beside it. Despite his physical frailties, he carried a deep sense of resilience. He was slender, bow-legged, and slightly kyphotic (meaning his spine was curved in a hunched posture), with a face marked by age and experience. His hearing was so impaired that I had to nearly shout to be heard. His old truck spoke of a life filled with challenges.

It was a privilege to care for Robert over the two years we got to know him. I loved that old man as if he were my own family. What stood out most was the compassion my office staff showed him. Robert struggled with reading and often brought in various forms, insurance papers, utility bills, and even his broken cell phone, for assistance. Christy, who worked at the front desk, and Melinda my nurse, took the time to help him with each document, patiently guiding him through the process. They went above and beyond, even feeding him during his visits when he had no other place to turn. He had very little, but he was always happy, and his heart was always full.

As Robert's health declined and he could no longer live alone, my Geriatric Fellow at the time, Dr. Hardin, took the lead in finding him a suitable nursing home. We continued to visit him to ensure he wasn't alone, providing the support and presence he needed. It was during these visits that we learned he had a family, though they were often absent.

On the day before Robert died, I sat beside him on his bed. Despite his weakness, he was happy to see me. We shared a silent understanding, just smiling at each other. I tried to feed him, but he wasn't interested. The next day, I returned to find him surrounded by his son, a hospice chaplain, and a few other family members. Robert was unresponsive, his breathing labored. I held his hand and, needing to attend to an urgent hospital consult, promised him I would be back. I told him it was okay to let go if he needed to.

I was gone for about two hours. When I returned, Robert passed away just five minutes later. It felt as though he had waited for me, a reminder of the trust and love we had built with him. My office staff, who had become his extended family, continued to show immense care and support. We had embraced him when his own family was not around, and in return, he had come to trust and love us deeply.

Robert's story is a powerful testament to the profound impact of compassion and empathy. It demonstrates that even in the absence of biological family, the human connections we forge through compassion can offer immense comfort and support. In our practice, we aim to extend this same level of compassion to every patient, ensuring they feel valued and cared for beyond their medical needs. Robert's journey through illness and care is just another example of how empathetic care can transform a patient's experience. The care team's dedication to understanding and addressing Robert's concerns, fears, and desires, despite his deteriorating condition, underscores the importance of maintaining a compassionate approach, even in the most challenging situations.

Compassion in medical care changes the narrative, reshapes the culture, and transforms the environment for patients. It places the patient at the center where they belong. Compassionate care helps pull a patient out of a place of fear and the unknown, bringing them into a space filled with hope and confidence. When fears are wiped away, patients can begin to heal. Ultimately, hope is what a patient needs to move forward. Medicine can be a scary place, but if we meet our patients in their fear and guide them out of it, we can truly help them heal.

Compassion is at the heart of medicine, often driving individuals to enter the field. However, as medical systems increasingly focus on efficiency and process, the personal touch of compassion can sometimes feel overshadowed. Despite these systemic challenges, preserving compassion remains essential for delivering effective and humane patient care. An example of this is when my partner, Dr. Kathleen Blaney, walked a patient and their family member to their car one day. The patient needed extra help, and as is common for geriatricians, Dr. Blaney went above and beyond to assist. When she returned to the office, she had tears in her eyes, deeply moved by the patient's and the family's struggles. Her emotional response highlighted her profound empathy and the enduring importance of compassionate care, even amidst the demands of a clinical environment.

The essence of compassion is beautifully captured in Dr. Wes Ely's book, "Every Deep-Drawn Breath," where Dr. Ely illuminates the profound impact of compassionate care in the medical field. As a seasoned pulmonary critical care doctor, Dr. Ely shares powerful narratives from the Intensive Care Unit, emphasizing how deeply empathetic care can transform patient outcomes and experiences. He argues that treating patients with genuine compassion, understanding their fears, hopes, and emotions, can foster healing in ways that go beyond the physical.

I read Dr. Ely's book during the COVID-19 pandemic, and I was deeply moved. At first, I was impressed by how a critical care doctor approached his patients. Taking a holistic approach is what geriatricians do, while everyone else often sticks to their lane: the cardiologist treats the heart, the nephrologist treats the kidneys, the pulmonary critical care doctor treats the lungs and keeps a patient alive, the surgeon cuts, and the neurologist treats the brain. While it often seems that way, that's not the full picture. There are doctors, like Dr. Ely, who understand and connect with the entire human being, recognizing that the body, mind, and our connection to life are deeply intertwined. Dr. Ely had saved his patients' stories and expanded on those, showing the importance of seeing the whole person.

Dr. Ely shares a powerful story about a patient who recounted their terrifying experience in the ICU. This patient described the fear and confusion they felt while sedated, and on a ventilator, which deeply impacted Dr. Ely. Hearing these experiences firsthand led him to re-evaluate his approach to critical care. He began to understand the detrimental effects of deep sedation and ICU delirium on patients' mental and physical health. This realization drove him to advocate for less sedation and more humane, patient-centered care practices. He started implementing protocols that involved keeping patients awake and alert when possible, and even promoting early mobility, such as walking patients while they were still on ventilators. These changes aimed to improve patient outcomes, reduce the incidence of delirium, and enhance the overall ICU experience.

ICU delirium is a serious and often overlooked condition characterized by acute confusion and disorientation that can occur in critically ill patients. It arises from a combination of factors, including severe illness, medication effects, and prolonged sedation. ICU delirium can lead to increased agitation, hallucinations, and long-term cognitive impairments. Not only does it prolong hospitalizations and complicate rehabilitation, but it also significantly increases the risk of death. The best approach is to prevent delirium whenever possible. Patients who experience delirium, especially older adults, are at a higher risk of developing long-term cognitive issues such as dementia. Preventive measures not only enhance immediate recovery but also help mitigate the risk of enduring cognitive decline.

During my time at the hospital, I was frequently called upon to see patients suffering from delirium. I even wrote a blog post on the subject and created a brochure to help family members support their loved ones during their hospital stay. The pandemic added another layer of difficulty; with visitation restrictions in place, many patients were isolated from their families, who were unable to be at their bedside.

As medical providers, we often appeared as blue-clad figures walking into patient rooms, while the patients remained alone for extended periods. This isolation was brutal, exacerbating the suffering of already vulnerable individuals. Families were understandably frustrated, and we, as healthcare workers, were overworked and exhausted. It was a time of unprecedented challenges, and the impact on patients, who were left without the comforting presence of their loved ones, was profound.

I felt an immediate connection to Dr. Ely's book because my own work had similarly focused on preventing delirium. Addressing this issue had been a central part of my practice when I rounded in the hospital, and seeing Dr. Ely's commitment to improving patient care through his innovative approaches resonated deeply with me. It reinforced the importance of compassionate, holistic care in every aspect of medicine, especially during such trying times.

In our practice, we strive to embody these principles. The compassion my staff showed Robert went beyond the medical care he received. It was in the way they helped him with his paperwork, fed him, and ensured he had a place to live. It was in the way we visited him and provided emotional support, making him feel like part of our family.

Ely's book underscores that this kind of compassionate care should extend to all our interactions, whether in medicine or everyday life. Compassion should be a fundamental part of how we treat each other, helping us build stronger, more empathetic communities. Robert's story is a testament to the profound impact of compassion, highlighting how even the smallest acts of kindness can make a significant difference in someone's life.

During the pandemic, while I was still serving as a geriatric program director, I had the incredible opportunity to meet Dr. Ely on a Zoom call. Dr. Ely was a guest speaker for a virtual weekly educational session organized by a program director at Vanderbilt. This session was a fantastic opportunity for fellows and faculty from across the United States and around the world to connect. Having recently read his book, I reached out to him via email, which led to a long and meaningful phone conversation. I expressed my gratitude for his book and mentioned that I was the writer of the blog Geriacademy.com, which he had referenced as a valuable resource on aging-related topics. Despite his busy schedule, Dr. Ely took the time to discuss his thoughts with me, and his words of encouragement were powerful as I shared my aspiration to write this book.

***

During the pandemic, the struggles I faced in caring for my patients were mirrored by my colleagues. One day, as I walked down the hospital hallway, I noticed a nurse who looked profoundly sad. Her eyes reflected a depth of sorrow that spoke volumes. At that moment, I didn't fully grasp the extent of her burden, but I was soon called in for a consult with a patient she was caring for. This patient, suffering from COVID, was in the final stages of life. His pre-existing dementia made it essential for his family to be present to help with basic needs, but due to pandemic restrictions, they could not be there.

As I evaluated the patient, who was severely delirious and in distress, I realized that discussing goals of care with him was impossible. Instead, I had to reach out to his family to explain the dire situation. Given the circumstances, I had to obtain special permission for the family to visit him as he approached the end of life. They made the difficult decision to transition to hospice care, allowing them to be with him during his final moments.

When I exited the room and spoke to the nurse, I saw the defeat in her eyes. Later that day, I learned that all four of the patients she was responsible for were critically ill, with a high likelihood of dying. Her exhaustion and sadness were palpable. I checked in with her again and asked if she was truly okay. Initially, she responded with a resigned "yes," as so many of us do when asked about our well-being. But when I pressed further, tears welled up in her eyes, and she admitted that she wasn't okay.

The COVID-19 pandemic highlighted the essential role of compassion in healthcare. Providers faced unprecedented challenges, including emotional exhaustion and moral distress. During this time, compassion became crucial not only for sustaining patient care but also for supporting provider well-being. The pandemic underscored the need for empathy as healthcare workers navigated the complexities of care under intense stress and isolation, reaffirming the value of a compassionate approach in maintaining morale and delivering quality care.

In that moment, I was reminded of the immense emotional toll of nursing, an often-thankless job where the dedication of nurses is paramount. They are the heart of medicine, connecting patients to the care they need and supporting doctors in their efforts. This experience highlighted for me the profound impact of compassion, not just in how we care for patients, but also in how we support each other in the demanding world of healthcare.

Nursing, at its core, is an embodiment of compassion and selflessness. Growing up, I witnessed this firsthand through my mother's dedicated approach to patient care. Her tender interactions and her willingness to work holidays so that younger nurses could be with their children were testaments to her deep empathy and commitment. She went above and beyond, not just caring for her patients but also supporting their families and the broader community. Although I didn't directly observe my mother-in-law's nursing career, I have seen her unwavering dedication as a caregiver, a reflection of her deep-rooted passion for nursing.

Nurses like my mother and mother-in-law not only provide critical support to their patients but also extend their compassion to the patients' families and the community. However, it is disheartening to see how nursing has evolved, with an increasing undervaluation of their true worth. The healthcare system often falls short in reciprocating the compassion that nurses provide. With rising staffing shortages and the departure of experienced nurses due to mounting pressures, there is a critical need for renewed appreciation and support. Nurses are the heart of compassionate care, and the system must recognize and sustain their invaluable contributions to patient care and the overall healthcare environment.

My journey through medical education was profoundly shaped by the support of nurses. The first six months of residency were particularly challenging as I grappled with navigating the hospital, writing orders, and understanding the complex dynamics of patient care. During this time, some of the nurses were instrumental in helping me adjust and grow. Their guidance and support provided a critical foundation for my development as a physician.

Similarly, in our practice, Tiffany, our nurse, is a cornerstone of our team. Her ability to address every problem, streamline processes, and provide calm support is invaluable. She not only helps our patients but also ensures the smooth operation of the office. Her presence brings a sense of reassurance and stability, allowing me to focus on providing the best care possible. I am deeply grateful for the pivotal role that nurses, like those who supported me in residency and Tiffany in our practice, have played in shaping who I am as a doctor. Their dedication and compassion are integral to our ability to deliver exceptional care. One day, Tiffany demonstrated her unwavering commitment to patient care in a way that truly exemplifies her dedication. She called me from a patient's home, where she had gone after our patient had fallen and sustained some cuts and scrapes. His family lived out of town, so Tiffany took it upon herself to visit him, clean and dress his wounds, and ensure he was safe and comfortable. She called me to update me on his condition and then followed up again after work to check on him.

Tiffany's willingness to make house calls, even though it's not part of her official job description, speaks volumes about her dedication. Her actions highlight the profound level of care she provides, attending to the whole patient, not just their medical needs, but their emotional and practical needs as well. Tiffany's commitment goes beyond the conventional boundaries of her role, embodying the true spirit of compassionate care. Her extraordinary efforts remind me of the vital role nurses play in patient care and how their dedication often goes unrecognized.

***

In reflecting on the stories and experiences shared in this chapter, it's clear that compassion is the cornerstone of effective and humane medical care. Dr. Ely's insights into critical care have illuminated the profound impact of treating patients as whole beings, addressing not only their physical but also their emotional and psychological needs. The pandemic has tested our limits, exposing the vulnerabilities of both patients and caregivers, yet it has also highlighted the extraordinary resilience and compassion that define our practice.

Through my own experiences, from dealing with ICU delirium to witnessing the tireless efforts of dedicated nurses like Tiffany, it's evident that the true heart of medicine lies in the connections we forge and the empathy we extend. Nurses, who often work behind the scenes, embody the spirit of selfless service, providing care that transcends mere medical intervention. Their contributions remind us that, despite the systemic challenges and undervaluation of their roles, their compassion remains an invaluable asset to our patients' well-being.

Compassion and empathy are not confined to the realm of medicine; they are fundamental to our humanity. They should be the root of all our interactions, shaping how we connect with one another and fostering a world where every individual feels seen, valued, and cared for. By integrating these principles into every facet of our lives, we honor the true meaning of human connection and ensure our actions reflect the dignity and respect that all people deserve. This approach not only enhances our practice but also contributes to a more compassionate and empathetic world.

In medicine, compassion is a cornerstone of effective care, enriching the doctor-patient relationship and improving patient outcomes. By embedding compassion into our practice, we not only elevate the quality of care but also affirm the human connection at the heart of healing. This chapter reaffirms that compassion is not merely a virtue but a vital component of meaningful care, influencing every aspect of the healing process.

I've emphasized these points throughout the chapter: while it may seem like I'm repeating myself, remember to be compassionate and have empathy. It is after all, the root of human connection.

Chapter 6

Creating Your Own Life, Without Expectations

Open wide the doors to your own happiness and sculpt the narrative of your life with grace. Let creativity guide you through the endless opportunities and unexpected surprises that life unfurls. Embrace the journey with an open heart, ever mindful of your true desires. Do it all with purpose and kindness!

"Dr. Sharafsaleh beats to her own drum." This comment from a patient was prominently displayed on my office wall and has always resonated with me. It captures the essence of my unconventional approach to medicine.

In October 2013, I embarked on my new role as an attending physician, a milestone that filled me with a mix of excitement and apprehension. For the first time, I was fully responsible for my patients' lives, with no attending physicians reviewing my work. Each decision, whether good or bad, rested on my shoulders, and the gravity of this responsibility was both thrilling and terrifying.

At that time, my life was a whirlwind of change. My husband was beginning a fellowship, and our two daughters, Mila and Zoey, were still quite young. Mila was three years old, full of energy and curiosity, while Zoey, just three months old, was the easiest baby I could have hoped for. They were in daycare, which allowed me to focus on my new job.

Reflecting on the moments that shape our lives and our family's story, I'm reminded of my three daughters, each with qualities that color our days in their own way. Zoey, with her boundless energy and ambition, lives each day with purpose and joy. Her dedication to gymnastics is evident in the steady thumps from the living room below as she practices backflips off her bed. Just as strong as her athletic drive is her creativity and persistence. Zoey doesn't simply ask for what she wants, she builds a case. We've sat through more than one of her elaborate PowerPoint presentations, complete with bullet points and persuasive arguments, on why we'd all be happier if we owned a snake or some other small rodent. When we refused to bring a snake home, she went searching for one herself. She came back announcing she'd found a large black snake and—before even catching it—had the nerve to ask if she could keep it. I had to tell her, quite clearly, that it was either me or the snake living in this house. As for the small furry rodents, we've had to gently explain that our dogs would likely turn that dream into a murder scene. Still, I can't help but admire Zoey's persistence, even when it drives us crazy. Her determination and imagination are part of what makes her who she is.

Mila, my oldest, much like her father, Jas, is grounded and focused. Her dedication to volleyball is unwavering, often involving long hours of practice and unconventional setups. Her determination has even led to broken windows from hitting balls against the walls and the occasional covert installation of a volleyball net in less-than-ideal spaces. Mila's rational approach and helpful nature shine through in the way she recognizes needs and steps in with thoughtful solutions. She often reflects on who she is, what she wants, and who she hopes to become. And somehow, when Mila wants something, she presents it so convincingly that it's hard to say no. She's not asking for snakes or furry creatures like her sister Zoey; instead, she builds a practical case for why she needs a new pair of shoes to improve her game or a better desk to study, though that desk may eventually turn into a vanity for her makeup. In these moments, I'm reminded of myself: I, too, have learned how to figure out what I need, what to say, and how to say it to get what I want. It's how I've built my life, always thoughtful, always adaptive.

Peyton, our youngest, with her impulsive and spontaneous spirit, brings a different kind of energy to our lives. She lives boldly, diving headfirst into new experiences and engaging with the world in a raw, unfiltered way. I often find myself challenged by her impulsivity. She creates vivid scenarios in her mind—how a conversation should unfold, how an experience is meant to go—and if reality doesn't match her vision, watch out, world. Yet, as our youngest, I can't help but believe this fierce imagination and determination may serve her well as she grows. With time and guidance, I hope she'll learn how to harness that passion, refine it, and channel it in a way that helps her build the life she envisions.

The apple doesn't fall far from the tree. Just as my daughters each carve out their own path, in 2013 I crafted my role as a physician with intention and creativity. During the job search, driven by our family's circumstances, I pitched a vision for my work, a combination of geriatric consultation and establishing a geriatric clinic at a retirement community. The job didn't exist until I proposed this idea, and thus, a new position was created.

Even though I initially focused on geriatrics, a part of me missed the broad scope of family medicine. So, for a time, I returned to practicing full-spectrum family medicine, which is how I ended up at the family medicine office in Lewisville, NC, where I remained until Jas completed his fellowship.

My husband's fellowship ended shortly after James had passed away, and I couldn't bear staying in the house any longer; I was eager for a change. I now remember that while Jas and I were interviewing for new jobs, I was pregnant with James. We knew about his illness, and people would congratulate me as they saw my large belly, oblivious to the deep pain those congratulations carried. They celebrated the impending arrival of a baby who was facing severe heart issues and a brief life. Despite the emotional turmoil, I maintained my composure, knowing I needed to stay focused and professional.

Practicing full-scope family medicine for a short time was enjoyable, but it also made me realize how much I needed to focus on geriatrics and aging. My interactions with elderly patients were far more meaningful, offering opportunities for self-growth and reflection. I came to understand that to truly make an impact as a doctor, I needed to commit to the field of geriatrics.

This decision was also driven by a pressing need in our healthcare system. According to the American Geriatrics Society, there are currently about 6,500 practicing geriatricians in the United States, while the demand is projected to require at least 30,000 to adequately serve our aging population. Each year, we train approximately 250 new geriatricians, but many of our current geriatricians are retiring, further exacerbating the shortage. With the U.S. population of older adults expected to double by 2030, this shortage poses a significant challenge. By dedicating myself to this field, I aimed to address this gap and provide the quality of care that our aging population deserves.

The interviewing process for my second job was quite revealing. Jas and I often found ourselves interviewing at the same hospitals or clinics in the same cities. During one interview, a CEO asked where I saw myself in five years. I explained that I envisioned a future where I contributed to geriatrics not only as a doctor but also in administrative and leadership roles to advance the field. The CEO, displaying a mix of arrogance and ignorance, dismissed my aspirations. He told me that doctors should stick to their clinical work and leave administrative tasks to others. Despite this, he offered me a job. More on this story later.

In contrast, Jas, who had interviewed at the same hospital, was highly sought after. They wined and dined us because they wanted him, presenting us with gift baskets and making various efforts to entice him. Meanwhile, I was treated dismissively and told by the CEO that I should remain in my place as a clinician. After my interview, I called Jas and told him he couldn't accept the offer because I would be miserable working there. Although he was interested in the position, he valued my career growth as a geriatrician and agreed with my assessment.

Jas then interviewed at a small community hospital in Morganton, NC, where I also had an interview. I was uncertain about how it would turn out. The Chief Medical Officer at the time, Dr. Mazzola, had a deep understanding of geriatrics. During our lengthy conversation, he immediately supported my goals. I shared my vision for the field: the need for more geriatricians, my desire to train them, and to inspire those in training to consider geriatrics. Dr. Mazzola wholeheartedly agreed with my vision. So again I started another position that did not exist and was created just for me, the way I had imagined it would be.

We are fortunate when facilities recognize the value of dedicated geriatric care and don't attempt to reassign geriatricians to internal medicine or family medicine roles, thereby disregarding their specialized training. This kind of recognition is crucial for advancing the field and ensuring that geriatricians can practice in their areas of expertise. I am profoundly grateful for Dr. Mazzola's support, which set me on a course to create the geriatric clinic and education program I had envisioned. I began training geriatricians according to my ideals.

While in Morganton, I embraced the opportunity to lead and innovate. During this time, I experienced a profound awakening regarding the business side of medicine. I realized that patient care and business often seemed misaligned, with financial considerations sometimes overshadowing patient-centered care. Although financial viability is important, I believed it was possible to provide excellent patient care while remaining profitable. To bridge this gap, I decided to pursue business school to gain a clearer understanding of what I needed to know.

Jas and I also delved into books on the business of medicine, with The Financially Intelligent Physician by Dr. David Norris being particularly influential for me. After reading his book, I reached out to Dr. Norris to discuss my considerations about business school. He strongly encouraged me to pursue it, sharing that it had been very helpful for him. I also spoke with him about my challenges of balancing full-time work and raising our children. He reassured me that he had managed similar challenges and believed I could too. This conversation reinforced my belief that medical training equips us with strength and the ability to tackle new challenges. While not everyone can be a doctor, any physician can certainly learn about business if they commit to it.

What intrigued me about Dr. Norris's book was its practical approach to managing finances within the context of a medical career. His concept of the 4 Ps—People, Productivity, Profitability, and Performance- resonated deeply with me. He demonstrated how these elements intertwine to shape effective leadership, financial intelligence, and operational effectiveness. Ultimately, these principles guide us towards exemplary patient care, illustrating that financial acumen and quality of care are not mutually exclusive but can enhance each other when thoughtfully integrated.

Jas decided to join me in this endeavor. For the next three years, we balanced full-time jobs, cared for our three children, and used the early mornings before they woke up and the nights after they went to bed to study. It was a challenging yet fulfilling journey. Upon completing business school, I came to a crucial realization: those who haven't been physicians or nurses should not make decisions affecting patient care. They do not belong in the C-Suite (C-Suite refers to executive roles like CEO, CFO, and COO). Conversely, physicians and nurses who lack a solid understanding of the business aspects of medicine should also not hold decision-making positions.

During this time, I was serving as the program director of the geriatric fellowship and had a non-traditional fellow, Dr. Kathleen Blaney. She was my age and had taken a break from medicine to take care of her three young children. Now, interested in geriatrics, she returned to the field. I often shared my frustrations with her and discussed how I envisioned a medical practice, and geriatric care should be delivered. As each semester of business school passed, I became increasingly aware of the shortcomings in our current process. Years later, after settling in Asheville, I reached out to Dr. Blaney. Together, we embarked on creating a practice that aligned with our vision: a place where patient care is at the center, and where we could balance our roles as mothers, entrepreneurs, and dedicated doctors.

As we later moved to Asheville, I took time to deeply reflect on what I wanted to achieve and how I wanted to achieve it. This period of introspection was not merely about career advancement but about aligning my professional aspirations with my personal values and vision. I considered the lessons I had learned and the experiences that had shaped me. Again, I created what I wanted and didn't settle.

In Asheville, I was determined to continue crafting a path that was uniquely my own. I sought out opportunities that resonated with my goals and allowed me to shape the field of geriatrics in a way that felt authentic and impactful. Whether it was through innovating new programs, advocating for patient-centered care, or developing leadership roles, I remained committed to forging my own route.

I've always marched to the beat of my own drum, choosing to follow my vision rather than the conventional path laid out before me. At times, that choice felt lonely and uncertain, but it also gave me the freedom to build a career deeply rooted in my passions and values. It wasn't the easiest road; there were moments of doubt and struggle yet staying true to myself allowed me to create work that felt meaningful and to touch the lives of my patients in ways that mattered deeply to me.

When I first decided to take the leap into private practice, my mother, who had always worked as a W-2 employee, was understandably concerned. She questioned whether I was making the right decision, especially given that I had a stable job with a good retirement plan and opportunities for growth. Despite the security of my current position, I felt confined and knew it wasn't aligned with my vision. During the 1970s and 1980s, medical education had promoted private practice as the ideal path for physicians, focusing on independence and entrepreneurship. However, as healthcare began shifting in the late 1990s towards employed positions within large systems, physicians increasingly found themselves treated as commodities, standardized and managed as interchangeable parts rather than valued individuals. This commodification often came with significant administrative pressures and a focus on productivity that could overshadow the essence of patient-centered care.

I was determined to see if my vision for a successful practice could still thrive amidst these changes. My drive to test my ideas and see them come to fruition was further fueled by dissatisfaction with my director, whose negative and arrogant attitude made the environment challenging. What kept me grounded was my role in undergraduate medical education, which provided me with protections and allowed me to balance teaching and clinical work. Having two bosses, one whom I greatly admired and one whose leadership I found lacking, made my decision to transition to private practice even more compelling. It offered me the autonomy and fulfillment I was seeking while allowing me to create a practice where patient care remained central, free from the constraints that had increasingly commodified employed physicians.

With my business degree in hand, I crafted a detailed business plan. My dear partner and friend, Dr. Kathleen Blaney, and I embarked on the journey to open our own practice. Although we were initially uncertain about many aspects, such as registering the business name, managing finances, and more, we were committed to figuring it out step by step.

Initially, we wanted to make our practice work within the confines of insurance billing, particularly Medicare. However, we soon realized that this approach was hindering our ability to deliver the quality care we envisioned. Medicare's regulations and reimbursements were not designed to support the kind of comprehensive, patient-centered care we wanted to provide. After much deliberation and research, we decided to transition to a concierge model, where patients pay a membership fee for enhanced access and personalized care. This model liberated us from the constraints of traditional practice and allowed us to focus entirely on patient care.

My practice model has allowed me to keep a small patient panel and focus on their health in a much deeper and meaningful way. It has allowed me to see my patients for 1-3 hours and discuss things that Medicare would not reimburse me for. For instance, I get to review a food and exercise diary that I have my patients fill out. I can go over what they like and what they don't like and within that create plans that are unique for them to increase their rate of success to achieve their health goals. I can motivate my patients and sit with them without rushing them out of the door so that I can see the next patient.

Honesty often finds its way into these relationships, sometimes in the most unexpected and endearing ways. During one visit, my patient Steve sat down and said, "Forgive me, Doctor, for I have sinned." I couldn't help but laugh. "You know," I told him, "That sounds like I'm your priest." He smiled and said, "Well, in a way, your kind of are." He went on to confess that he hadn't been following my advice and neglecting his goals. With a mix of humor and self-awareness, he admitted, "I'm my own worst enemy, I always seem to find a way to sabotage my health." I told him that, as his physician-priest, all I could do was bless him with good health tips and the hope he'd put them to use. We both laughed, and before leaving, he smiled and said, "I'm only human."

That kind of honesty, coupled with trust, forms the foundation of healing. It reminds me that care is not about perfection but about connection—meeting people where they are, even when they falter. Steve wasn't making excuses; he was simply acknowledging who he was. He admitted to being human and fully aware that this was the life he had created for himself, with all its flaws, choices, and lessons.

Throughout my career as a geriatrician, the stories of my patients have been my inspiration. Their journeys have encouraged me to persevere, to pick up, get up, and keep going. Not just to keep going, but to do what you love. My most successful patients are those who have created their own paths, who didn't just settle for what life handed them. They fought back for what was right and what they wanted, not letting failures or challenges stand in their way.

Colleen is one of these success stories. She found me after reading *Elderhood: Redefining Aging, Transforming Medicine, Reimagining Life* by Dr. Louise Aronson, a book that challenges negative stereotypes associated with aging and calls for a transformation in how society and the medical profession treat older adults. When Colleen first came to my office, she explained that she was transitioning from her condominium to a home closer to her son due to some health issues. Despite struggling with balance and significant hip pain, Colleen had embraced a new approach to her health. She began exercising regularly, worked with a personal trainer, and became stronger than she had been in years. Her trainer reported that Colleen was doing deadlifts and box jumps. Determined to take control of her health, Colleen had read *Elderhood* not just once but twice, underlining passages that spoke to her sense of agency and possibility.

But what makes Colleen's story remarkable is that her transformation extended beyond physical health. She chose to address all aspects of aging, body, mind, and spirit. Colleen is deeply rooted in her community: she remains an active member of her church and participates in her town's oldest book club, where she finds joy in learning and conversation. She helps raise her grandson, picking him up after school and planning activities together, creating the kind of intergenerational connection that keeps her both grounded and vibrant. She focuses on a well-balanced diet, staying socially engaged, and nurturing her emotional well-being. Colleen doesn't just strive to live longer; she strives to live better. Her focus is not simply on lifespan but on health-span, on the quality, connection, and meaning within the years she has.

***

One year, at an American Geriatrics Society meeting, I attended a session for program directors where I had the chance to meet Dr. Louise Aronson. During our conversation, Dr. Aronson shared that she was about to publish a book. Curious, I asked her about it, and she responded, "Elderhood." When I looked puzzled, she explained, "You know, childhood, adulthood, and elderhood." Her insight struck me as brilliant, and I promised to buy the book and have it signed the following year.

Unfortunately, the pandemic interrupted those plans, and my first edition remains unsigned. However, as I read *Elderhood*, I felt as though Dr. Aronson was articulating my own thoughts and vision for geriatric medicine. Her exploration of elderhood as a distinct and meaningful phase of life resonated deeply with me and reaffirmed my commitment to practicing in a way that honors the complexity and dignity of older patients.

Before *Elderhood*, Atul Gawande's *Being Mortal* was the most influential book I had encountered on geriatric care. Gawande's work was groundbreaking, shedding light on the limitations of modern medicine and emphasizing the importance of quality of life over mere longevity. It deeply resonated with my experiences in the field. And perhaps I loved it a little more because, for once, someone had recognized just how important geriatricians truly are.

Elderhood expanded and enriched these conversations. Inspired by Dr. Aronson's work, I now regularly give a copy of *Elderhood* to my patients. When we begin our conversations, I frame it this way: "You've had your childhood and adulthood. Now, let's focus on this incredible phase, your elderhood. This is a time when you are no longer just navigating the world, figuring out how to care for yourself, or managing the responsibilities of raising children and working. Instead, elderhood is an opportunity to reflect, grow, and explore a lifetime of experiences and your purpose on this earth. It's a time for new experiences and liberation from the confines of earlier life stages."

This perspective on elderhood has been liberating for many of my patients, offering them a new way to view this phase of their lives. It underscores that elderhood is not just a period of decline but a time of profound potential and exploration. However, it's worth noting that while the book's message is empowering, it also presents a brutally honest portrayal of aging. Embracing aging, which is something society has often struggled to do, can be a challenging shift in perspective. For some of my older patients, this candid depiction of the complexities and challenges of aging may feel overwhelming or even sad. Yet, for me, it has been a source of inspiration, pushing me to embrace the fullness of elderhood and advocate for a more compassionate and effective approach to care.

***

Dawn had been her husband's caregiver, completely devoted to ensuring all his needs were met. When I met her, her husband required complete care—and he towered over her. Dawn was barely 4'11" and weighed around 98 pounds, petite but strong in spirit. Her husband, by contrast, was well over six and a half feet tall, and I often marveled at how she managed to help him physically when he needed so much support. Her devotion was unwavering; she wanted to ensure he lived the best life possible, despite the enormous physical and emotional demands of caregiving. After her husband passed away, Dawn didn't know how to move forward without being a caregiver and missed him deeply. Yet even in her grief, she understood that she needed to find meaning in her life without him. Through her clarity and optimism, she eventually found love again.

Time and time again, I met patients who shared their stories of finding new beginnings and achieving what they wanted. Charles refused to accept a terminal diagnosis of advanced prostate cancer and give up. Instead, he researched and found treatment that allowed him to survive years past his expected time. One of my dear patients Robin started skiing at 40 years old, participating in activities that her children enjoyed so she could be present for them. Dorothy, who lost two of her adult children and endured an abusive first marriage, was determined to be healthy and strong, and she succeeded.

Chris, diagnosed with dementia, came into my office one day and told me he wanted to go to Switzerland. For a doctor, especially a geriatrician, this often means seeking physician-assisted suicide. Switzerland is one of the few countries that allow a person with dementia to make this choice. Chris wanted to live on his own terms and not let the disease take over. His partner Tricia understood and supported him. He knew that advanced dementia would mean losing his ability to walk, eat, recognize loved ones, and engage in the activities that gave his life meaning. He wanted his death, too, to be on his own terms, just as he had lived as a civil rights attorney, father, and friend.

I learned that we have the power to create our own lives the way we want them to be. It's about taking chances, believing in ourselves, and trusting our instincts. We must forge our paths without rigid expectations, understanding that life's unpredictability can lead to unexpected opportunities and growth. By embracing this mindset, I was able to craft a fulfilling career and personal life, even when it meant stepping away from conventional roles and security.

My journey continues, with doors closing and new opportunities arising. The key is to remain open and continually ask myself, "What is it that I really want?" and then go after that. It's never too late to learn something new, reinvent ourselves, or change course if what we're doing isn't working out. This approach has taught me that while we can't control every outcome, we can control our efforts and stay true to our desires, adapting and growing with each step we take.

As we marvel at the feats of athletes and public figures who push the boundaries of human capability, we often forget that true heroes may be closer to home than we realize. Our grandparents, parents, and elders are the unsung champions whose lives are filled with remarkable stories of courage and perseverance. They have faced challenges, navigated adversity, and achieved personal victories that can inspire and guide us if we take the time to listen.

Imagine sitting down with an elder, not just as a family member but as a source of wisdom and inspiration. Through their stories, we can gain insights into the struggles they have overcome, the dreams they have pursued, and the lessons they have learned. Their experiences, though sometimes less visible than a sports record or a public achievement, are filled with profound truths about what it means to live fully and with purpose.

By engaging with our elders and learning from their journeys, we open ourselves to a richer understanding of life. Their tales of triumphs and trials can teach us not only about perseverance but also about the power of hope and endurance. They remind us that even in the face of difficulty, there is always something to strive for, something to learn, and something to cherish.

So, let us take a moment to sit down with those who have come before us, to hear their stories and learn from their experiences. In doing so, we not only honor their lives but also enrich our own, drawing strength from their wisdom and allowing their legacy to inspire us as we forge our own paths.

In embracing this perspective, we acknowledge that our heroes are not just the athletes or public figures who capture our attention but also the elders who have quietly shaped our lives with their courage, wisdom, and love.

Chapter 7

The Spirit's Triumph: Navigating Life's Trials with Strength and Hope

Through the depths of our struggles and the journey of rising from them, we uncover the true measure of our strength and the profound power that lies within us.

Growing up, I faced challenges that were different from those of many of my peers. Although I was born in the U.S., my family's journey took us back to Iran after the revolution and then back to the States. This return was not straightforward. My father had to come first, leaving my mother to navigate our lives with my younger sister and me, aged six and four, in Vienna.

Vienna, a far cry from the lavish life we had left behind,

became our unexpected home for nearly two years. When we first arrived, we stayed in a hotel, believing our time there would be brief, a few weeks at most before we joined my father in America. But weeks turned into months. My mother shared one small room with my sister and me, doing her best to create a sense of normalcy amid constant uncertainty. Each morning, we joined other guests in the breakfast room, people who came and went while we remained, our lives suspended. My mother tried repeatedly to secure a permanent visa to the United States, but every attempt ended the same way: a temporary visit visa she didn't want to risk accepting. My aunt Jan, an immigration attorney, flew back and forth from the U.S. to help us, yet every door seemed to close just as another cracked open. We made our way back to the United States when I was almost nine. Without Aunt Jan's tireless determination, the life I've lived and the story I'm able to tell now would not exist. I would be writing a completely different book.

Eventually, our savings ran out, and my mother had no choice but to leave the hotel. I remember walking through the streets of Vienna with our suitcases, my mother's face tight with worry as she searched for a place for us to stay. We spent one night in another small hotel before she found a young man renting a room in his modest apartment. For a while, that became our home. My mother's strength began to wear thin, and I could sense her exhaustion. Just as she was starting to lose hope, something remarkable happened.

While we had lived in the first hotel, we'd befriended a kind man named Mr. Gigi, who had family in Russia but couldn't return due to political unrest. One day, as we walked the streets trying to figure out what to do next, we saw him again, by pure chance. He was living in an apartment building that belonged to a doctor and invited us to meet him. That meeting changed everything. The doctor offered my mother a room to rent and later work caring for his elderly mother, which gave her enough income to cover food and school for us. For the first time in months, my mother allowed herself to exhale.

By then, she had let go of the idea that we would return to the U.S. anytime soon. She enrolled my sister and me in school; it had been over a year since we'd last attended. I began to learn German and to see Vienna not as a temporary stop but as a place where life continued. My mother, ever resourceful, found ways to stretch every dollar, cooking simple meals and finding small joys where she could.

And then, that winter, Mr. Gigi surprised us with something unforgettable. He introduced us to Christmas. He brought a small tree to our apartment and placed two gifts underneath it—one for my sister and one for me. I still remember the thrill of unwrapping a little handheld video game, primitive by today's standards, but to me, it was magic. It was the first toy I'd had in a very long time. That small act of kindness, the gift, the laughter, the warmth—became one of my earliest lessons in hope and humanity.

Despite the hardships, Vienna became a place of unexpected triumph. My mother's determination never wavered. Through her resilience, the compassion of strangers, and a few small miracles, she found a way to keep us safe and together. Looking back now, I see that those years—though filled with uncertainty—taught me what strength truly means.

Growing up, I was accustomed to hearing stories of immigrants and their trials, each one a testament to fortitude and perseverance. My Aunt Maryam, for instance, arrived in the U.S. with nothing and faced immense challenges, working two full-time jobs while attending pharmacy school despite the exhaustion and the burden of out-of-state tuition. These stories of family, friends, cousins, and acquaintances shaped who I became and who I am today. Alongside Aunt Maryam's narrative, the story of Dr. Mehra, who returned to Iran to help develop Namazee Hospital into a leading research and medical center, became integral to my understanding of life's difficulties. Their experiences taught me that while life is hard, it is through facing these challenges head-on that we truly grow and thrive. This ingrained lesson instilled in me the belief that perseverance and a steadfast attitude are key to overcoming adversity and has profoundly shaped my approach to life and its challenges.

I met Dr. Mehra later, during my college years, when I also met his grandson, Narsy, the first man I ever fell in love with. He was young, kind, and, at the time, perfect in my eyes. His smile lifted me up, and his easy-going nature made me feel seen in a way I hadn't before. He had a way of saying yes to life, ready to jump into whatever idea I had, no matter how impulsive or impractical. Maybe that's why I fell for him, not just for who he was, but for the family he came from, a family that radiated warmth, laughter, and an effortless joy in living.

Those years with him were filled with firsts. We climbed mountains, sometimes literally, hiking and camping in places that felt like the middle of nowhere. I had never been someone who liked to get dirty, yet with him, I didn't mind sleeping in a tent or cooking over a small fire. We went dancing every chance we got, wild, unrestrained nights when time felt infinite and the music never seemed to end. For the first time, I felt completely free, as if the world had opened up and I was learning who I really was outside of family expectations, outside of the plans that had been laid out for me.

We went skydiving, speeding down highways with the windows open, the wind in our faces, laughing as if life itself were daring us to dream bigger. It was that fleeting moment in youth when you believe you're invincible, untouchable, until you realize you never truly are. But that illusion of invincibility, that raw rush of being alive, leaves an imprint. It teaches you what it means to be fearless, even if only for a little while.

His family welcomed me as their own. They were full of joy and energy, the kind of family that celebrated everything: birthdays, milestones, and even the smallest victories. I remember his grandmother's laughter, the smell of food drifting through the house, and the feeling that there was always room at the table for one more person. To be embraced by that kind of love, after all the instability of my childhood, was healing in ways I didn't recognize then. It taught me that family didn't have to mean blood; sometimes it was simply the people who opened their doors and hearts to you.

But as life goes, we grow up, we grow apart, and we move on. Love doesn't always end in heartbreak; sometimes it ends because our paths diverge, and we are called toward something different. For me, that calling was medicine. Leaving Salt Lake City and Narsy was one of the hardest choices I've ever made, but it was also one of the most defining. I left to follow a dream, a purpose, a vision of service that had been growing inside me for years. And in doing so, I discovered that life could expand far beyond what I had imagined with him.

Still, I'm deeply grateful that the powers that be brought

him and his family into my life for that chapter of my journey. He was my first great love, and through him, I learned that love can be both an anchor and a launching point, that sometimes the very thing that steadies you is also what gives you the courage to leap.

Spending time with Dr. Mehra helped me begin to see the Iran my mother and father often spoke about, the country that felt almost like a dream to me growing up. Until then, her stories had been pieces of another world: the tree-lined streets of Shiraz, its jasmine-scented evenings, the laughter that filled their gatherings, and the pride she felt in being part of a modern, educated society. Through Dr. Mehra, I started to understand what that life must have been like. He carried himself with the same dignity and optimism my parents described in the people of their youth, a generation that believed in progress, in education, in building something meaningful for their country.

Dr. Mehra often spoke about *Namazee Hospital*, where he had served as medical director before returning to the United States. The way he described it made it clear that it was more than a hospital, it was a vision for what Iran could become. In the 1960s and 70s, Shiraz was one of the most advanced and Western-influenced cities in the Middle East, home to universities, thriving art and music, and a medical community eager to learn from and collaborate with the West. Namazee hospital stood at the center of that progress, equipped with cutting-edge technology and staffed by physicians trained in Europe and the U.S. who had returned home to elevate medicine in their own country.

Listening to him, I realized that medicine, for people like Dr. Mehra and my mother's generation, was more than a career, it was a calling, a way to serve, to rebuild, and to move a nation forward. His stories connected me not only to my cultural roots but also to the spirit of service that defined both my family and the Iran they once knew. It was through him that I began to understand how deeply medicine was woven into my heritage, how it symbolized resilience, hope, and progress.

Our walks together and his stories deepened my resolve to pursue a medical career. His experiences, along with those of my Aunt Maryam, taught me that while life is undeniably hard, it is within these hardships that true beauty and growth emerge. Facing challenges head-on is not merely a struggle but a journey that reveals our strength and potential. This profound lesson, that perseverance and strength are key to overcoming adversity, and that hardship itself can be a beautiful part of our growth, has profoundly shaped my approach to life and the challenges it presents.

Watching my mother face these hardships with courage and determination taught me invaluable lessons about attitude and resilience. Despite the difficulties, she managed to maintain hope and a sense of purpose, which ultimately shaped our journey. Her ability to adapt and persevere through such trying times highlighted the profound impact of a positive attitude. Even so, my mother's strength didn't exist in isolation, she drew energy from those who loved her most, her children, her family, and especially her sister, Mali.

Later, as an adult, I understood why my mother encouraged us to be so close to each other. She had the same relationship with her sisters, especially her younger sister, Mali. Despite their differences, they shared a deep and supportive bond. Mali, who was like a mother to me, always had a cup full of encouragement and motivation. She was a source of strength for my mother, lifting her spirits when she felt down and offering unwavering support through the hardest times. This close-knit relationship between my mother and her sister Mali illuminated for me the importance of having a supportive family connection and how such bonds can help us navigate the challenges of life with grace and strength.

My mother and her sister spoke on the phone every single day, without fail. They knew each other's secrets, shared their innermost thoughts, and carried each other's hearts. For 73 years, my mother's closest friend was her sister. When my aunt passed away, my mother was by her side, holding her hand in those final moments. I captured a photograph of my mother grasping her sister's hand after she had passed. I often look at that picture, reflecting on the profound love they shared and the strength they drew from each other. It serves as a powerful reminder of their deep bond and the lifetime of memories they built together.

In the aftermath of my aunt's death, my mother struggled with feelings of guilt for surviving her sister. My uncle, who was much older than my aunt, also wrestled with the same feelings of confusion and sorrow. Both have found it difficult to reconcile why their younger sister passed away before them, leaving a void that neither has been able to fully understand or accept.

My Aunt Mali's story is also one of triumph and determination. She and her husband relocated their family to the U.S., working tirelessly for everything they achieved. Life was challenging, and they often faced hardships, but they succeeded in raising their three children. Both my mother and my aunt imparted to us the wisdom of valuing family, persevering through difficult times, and always rising above challenges. They taught us the importance of never giving up, of picking ourselves up, and continuing to move forward no matter the obstacles.

These were the lessons I absorbed throughout my life: to stand by your sister's side, to stay close to your family, and to treat your cousins as if they are your siblings. The most important lesson was to be present for one another. In their old age, my mother and my aunt taught me the true value of family bonds and the strength found in unwavering support. Luckily, I married a man whose mother is the eternal optimist. Her belief in the power of family and her unwavering positivity reinforced the values I learned from my own family, reminding me of the profound impact of sticking together and facing life's challenges with a hopeful attitude.

Through all the ups and downs, my sister has been an unwavering source of strength and support. Despite being younger, she has often shown remarkable wisdom beyond her years. She was by my side on my wedding day, and I was honored to stand by her during hers. She has always been more than just a sibling; she is my advisor, my confidante, and my rock. Her ability to remain strong and insightful, even when I falter, underscores the profound bond we share. Our relationship is a testament to the power of having someone who truly understands and supports you through every moment, whether joyful or challenging.

How we handle bad news and navigate through life's challenges can profoundly affect our journey. Resilience plays a critical role in helping us grow old. I often joke with my patients that reaching old age requires toughness, getting old is not for the faint of heart. It's a truth that resonates deeply, as we know that the weak often fall away, while resilience allows us to persist and find strength even in the darkest times.

This was vividly illustrated in Joe's story. Hands clasped tightly, eyes reflecting fear, Joe asked, "So is it Alzheimer's or dementia?" I proceeded to explain that Alzheimer's is just a type of dementia and provided him with as much information as he could handle that day. It was clear that Joe needed to wrap his mind around this new reality. His wife, Lydia, sat next to him, struggling to hold back tears. Her eyes, filled with anguish, darted between Joe and me. It felt as though I had delivered a death sentence. Though I couldn't cure Joe's condition or halt its progression, his response was surprisingly optimistic.

Joe wanted to understand the timeline and progression of his disease. I looked at him and then at Lydia, trying to gauge how much to reveal. Lydia's widening eyes silently warned me to tread carefully. I aimed to break the news gently while respecting Joe's dignity. At the time of his diagnosis, Joe had mild to moderate dementia, functioning at a mental age of around 7-10. Despite his cognitive decline, his spirit remained unbroken.

He was scared, repeatedly asking the same questions, perhaps hoping for a different answer. The harsh reality was that Joe would gradually lose more skills, driving, managing finances, using a phone, and eventually even basic activities like eating and walking. He would become fully dependent, facing complications such as aspiration pneumonia and infections. His physical decline would include contractures in his hands and feet, skin breakdown, and ultimately a slow drift toward the end. How could I convey this bleak future to him? How could I explain that everything he had worked for and the retirement he had envisioned with Lydia was slipping away? I couldn't fully reveal the harshness of what lay ahead. Instead, I focused on helping him process things gradually, knowing that as his awareness diminished, his concerns about the disease would lessen. Through it all, Joe's determination and willingness to confront his reality demonstrated his true strength. My hope was that Lydia's strength, faith, and the support of their family would help them navigate this challenging journey together.

Lydia's unwavering dedication was evident. She managed Joe's care with remarkable devotion, constantly worrying about his well-being, even when he visited their son. Her concern extended to every detail of his care, ensuring he didn't get lost, that he ate enough, and that his needs were met. Her own well-being seemed to take a backseat as she devoted herself to Joe. I often wondered if she fully appreciated her own strength and the immense burden she carried. A research project I conducted with a geriatric fellow revealed that caregivers, particularly spouses, often exhibit greater resilience and better coping skills compared to adult children. However, caregivers can sometimes become ill themselves due to neglecting their own needs. This insight reinforced my commitment to supporting both Joe and Lydia. I needed to ensure that Lydia's well-being was safeguarded as much as Joe's, to help her navigate the demands of caregiving without becoming overwhelmed.

I saw this unwavering love and support from another patient of mine in the past. At the age of 80, Pat was a Methodist minister who had served three churches and was also a published author. Her husband, who was afflicted with dementia, became increasingly dependent on her care. Pat tended to him for as long as she could, but as his condition worsened, the challenges became overwhelming. He would wander, forget where he was, and struggle to recognize those around him. The breaking point came when he swung a golf club at someone on a golf course, unable to comprehend the situation. Despite her deep reluctance and emotional struggle, Pat knew that placing him in a nursing home was the only viable option left. She was utterly exhausted from tending to his every need while trying to hold onto any sense of self she had left.

Despite the profound loss and struggle, Pat moved forward with remarkable inner strength. She continued to pursue the work she was so passionate about, carrying on with her writing and ministry. Even after her husband passed away, she remained dedicated to her calling. During one of our last conversations, she mentioned considering slowing down and retiring, reflecting on the next chapter of her life. Her commitment to her work and her ability to find purpose even in the face of such personal trials was a testament to her strength and enduring spirit.

As I've come to witness, caregiving requires an extraordinary depth of strength and fortitude. It's not just about the physical demands but also the emotional and psychological toll that accompanies this role. The challenges of caregiving can be immense, and the burden often goes unrecognized, manifesting in feelings of hopelessness, depression, or even aggression. Yet, much like the biblical David, caregivers often find themselves facing their own Goliaths, seemingly insurmountable challenges that require them to adapt in ways they never anticipated.

But even with all the resilience and adaptability in the world, caregivers often face another, quieter battle, one that unfolds in the privacy of their own thoughts. Guilt has a way of creeping in, no matter how much love or effort they give. I was reminded of this during a recent conversation with one of my patient's husbands, Ross, who has been caring for his wife, Jayne, as she lives with dementia. He told me there's a difference between static guilt, the kind that keeps you stuck, unable to grow or heal, and transformative guilt, the kind that asks, what is life trying to teach me through this? "He said, the difference is whether you see this as punishment or as an opportunity." When you're confronted with something hard, do you get stuck in it, or do you let it help you grow?"

His words made me think about how caregivers often become "paralysed by guilt," feeling that no matter what they do, it's never enough. He described waking in the middle of the night thinking, *How am I going to do this?*- the endless cycle of worry and responsibility that can consume a person's spirit.

As he spoke, I pictured an image in my mind: a person holding out their hands while books are stacked one after another, each one representing guilt, obligation, and unspoken fear. At first, it's manageable, but slowly the stack grows taller and heavier until it blocks their view, rising above their head, pressing down on their arms, weighing on their chest. They can no longer see what lies ahead, yet they still try to hold on to every book. That's what caregiving looks like when it becomes static, when the burden eclipses the light.

But if we can begin to set those books down, one at a time, what's hidden slowly comes back into view. The weight lightens, and in its place comes space for learning, for healing, and for love. That is the essence of growth: the moment we stop seeing adversity as punishment and start seeing it as life asking us to rise.

In these moments, the ability to adapt to circumstances becomes a vital skill. Just as David's unconventional approach allowed him to triumph against the giant, caregivers often discover hidden strengths and resources within themselves. They learn to navigate the unpredictable terrain of caregiving, finding new ways to manage the emotional and physical toll. This adaptability is not merely about surviving the day-to-day tasks; it's about transforming the caregiving journey into one of resilience and growth, even in the face of overwhelming odds.

I have witnessed caregivers demonstrate remarkable tenacity and adaptability in their roles, often navigating emotional and physical challenges with unwavering grace. Their ability to endure and navigate the challenges of caregiving, despite their own limitations, never ceases to amaze me. Studies reveal that nearly 50% of caregivers are themselves aged 65 or older, and many of them manage significant health issues while providing care.

However, the struggles of caregivers often go unnoticed. They face an immense burden, which can lead to severe consequences for their own health and well-being. According to the National Alliance for Caregiving and AARP, 40% of family caregivers report their health has worsened due to caregiving responsibilities. This strain can lead to increased rates of chronic illness, depression, and even premature mortality.

Caring for caregivers is equally crucial, yet their needs are often overlooked. The exhaustion and stress they endure are rarely addressed, and their own health issues are frequently missed. Tragically, I have witnessed instances where caregivers, despite their unwavering commitment, have passed away before the loved ones they were tending to. This stark reality underscores the importance of recognizing and addressing the toll caregiving takes on these individuals, ensuring that their own health and needs are not sidelined in the process of caring for others. By providing caregivers with appropriate support, resources, and respite, we can help them maintain their health and continue to offer care with the strength and dignity they so richly deserve.

Reflecting on my own experiences, I am reminded of when I was 16 and saw my mother's dedication in caring for my grandfather, who had dementia. I watched her help him with baths, feed him, and manage the numerous aspects of his care. Her selflessness and strength were deeply inspiring and left a lasting impression on me. This personal experience reinforced the significance of acknowledging and supporting caregivers, recognizing the immense emotional and physical demands they face.

Our culture often places elderly individuals in nursing homes or assisted living facilities, creating spaces like retirement communities that separate us generationally. This segmentation can lead us to miss out on the richness of experiencing the full spectrum of life together. By distancing ourselves from the elderly, we not only lose sight of the profound truth that humanity thrives on mutual responsibility, but we also miss seeing the incredible strength and resilience that elders often embody. Instead of viewing them as robust and capable, we might perceive them as weak, failing to appreciate the remarkable fortitude they display.

Malcolm Gladwell, in his book *David and Goliath*, explores the idea that what may seem like disadvantages can often be hidden strengths. This perspective is essential when considering how we care for our elderly. It's not solely the task of strangers to care for us; rather, it should be a shared duty among families, friends, and neighbors, driven by empathy and mutual support. This sense of collective responsibility is a fundamental aspect of human connection. By embracing this responsibility within our own circles, we not only enrich our lives but also honor the integral role each of us plays in nurturing and supporting one another through all stages of life.

Having had the honor of witnessing the strengths of unsung heroes in the face of adversity, through the experiences of my patients, family, and friends, has profoundly shaped my understanding of resilience. These encounters have taught me the importance of picking up the pieces after life's inevitable setbacks and pushing forward with renewed determination. But this lesson wasn't just something I learned from others; it's a lesson I had to learn myself, through my own struggles.

When I first started medical school, I was unprepared for the immense challenges that lay ahead. With a background in behavioural science and gerontology, I wasn't used to the rigorous demands of medical training. My first semester was difficult, I was lonely, barely surviving, and by the second semester, it all caught up to me. I failed physiology, and in that moment, I felt like my dream of becoming a doctor was over. I returned home, devastated and ready to give up. Despite wanting more than anything to be a doctor, I was convinced that I was done.

I vividly remember sitting in my mother's room, in tears, feeling like a failure with no way forward. But then my aunt, who was a physician herself, came over to talk to me. She saw something in me that I couldn't see in myself at the time. She told me, firmly but lovingly, that I was going to go back, repeat the semester, and move on. She believed in me when I didn't believe in myself. So, I went back.

I realized that my struggles were not just about the material, I had ADHD, and I was so distracted that I needed to retrain myself on how to study, how to think, how to approach learning. I had to completely recreate the way I studied and processed information. It was a humbling experience, but it taught me that failure is not the end; it's a part of the journey. It's an opportunity to adapt, to find new strategies, and to grow stronger.

This understanding of resilience has only deepened in my experience as a faculty member. I am continually impressed by the strength and determination of medical students, residents, and fellows, especially my female colleagues. Navigating the demands of motherhood while excelling in a demanding profession is no small feat. I see this strength in my partners and colleagues, who balance the challenges of being both dedicated doctors and loving mothers. Their ability to adapt, persevere, and thrive in the face of overwhelming demands is nothing short of inspiring.

Just like those who have defied expectations throughout my life, and just like I had to in my own journey, these women embody strength. They remind me that resilience is not just about enduring challenges, but about finding new ways to overcome them, even when the odds are stacked against you.

The ability to reframe life's challenges is not just a survival mechanism but a transformative process that builds inner strength. As Friedrich Nietzsche famously wrote, "That which does not kill us makes us stronger." This idea, echoed in the popular saying "what doesn't kill you makes you stronger," resonates deeply with me. It's a reminder that the struggles we endure are not merely obstacles but opportunities to grow, adapt, and emerge stronger than before.

But resilience isn't just about enduring hardship; it's also about adapting to new realities and finding alternative paths when our original plans are no longer possible. This concept is beautifully explored in Sheryl Sandberg's book *Option B*. After the sudden death of her husband, Sandberg was forced to confront the painful truth that the life she had envisioned, her "Option A", was no longer attainable. She had to find a way to move forward, to redefine success, and to build a new life for herself and her children. *Option B* is a powerful testament to the human capacity to adapt, to find new options when life takes an unexpected turn, and to thrive even in the face of overwhelming loss.

In observing those around me, I've seen how adversity can reveal hidden reserves of strength and resilience. Patients facing terminal illnesses, family members overcoming personal crises, and friends navigating their own battles have shown me that true strength lies not just in enduring hardship but in adapting to it. Their experiences have illustrated that while we may face moments of profound loss or upheaval, it is our capacity to reframe and redefine our paths that truly determines our growth.

When life forces us to abandon our original plans, we are presented with an opportunity to explore "Option B", to find new ways to succeed, to redefine what it means to thrive, and to embrace the possibility that, despite the loss of what was, there is still potential for growth and renewal. This mindset embodies the essence of Nietzsche's "will to power," where our drive for achievement and creativity becomes a source of strength in the face of adversity.

By embracing this mindset, we not only survive our challenges but also thrive in the face of them. We continually evolve and grow stronger with each hurdle we overcome, often discovering that hardship leads to a deeper understanding of ourselves and our capacity to adapt. In this way, adversity becomes not a barrier to our success but a catalyst for our transformation, enabling us to find new meaning and purpose in the ever-unfolding narrative of our lives.

Chapter 8

Adapting & Embracing Change with A Mad Scientist's Spirit

"It is only with the heart that one can see rightly; what is essential is invisible to the eye." Antoine de Siant-Exupéry *The Little Prince*

Sit and rest, for you have journeyed far. This world has unveiled doors you never sought, while closing those you longed to keep ajar. You have gracefully crafted and adapted to each season's turn. Now, it is time to rest and reflect on the beauty you've earned.

In the high-stakes world of patient care, I often feel like a mad scientist grappling with a complex, malfunctioning machine that represents my patients' conditions. Picture me in a big apron and oversized plastic gloves, standing before a chaotic contraption straight out of a 70s sci-fi movie. This machine—an intricate system of symptoms, anatomic failures, and stubborn imaging—has endless valves and tangled hoses. With each adjustment, whether analyzing a problem lab result, imaging like a brain MRI, or deciphering disjointed symptoms, I'm in a frantic race against time. The urgency I feel is sometimes met with a disheartening lack of immediacy from the specialists I consult, not because specialists don't care, but because the bond I have with these patients is different. As I sweat and strain, frantically turning knobs and pulling levers, I'm driven by the hope of bringing comfort and resolution. Despite my best efforts, there are moments when I feel as if I've failed, battling the complexities of each patient's condition with the determination of a scientist trying to make a breakthrough.

Now, I must admit that as a geriatrician, my work isn't as intense as that of my husband, who is a pulmonary critical care doctor or of a surgeon. I often tell my kids that Daddy literally saves lives with his hands, while I'm the one who thinks, and thinks, and thinks some more, piecing together the puzzle and coordinating with specialists to get my patients the care they need.

But sometimes that thinking doesn't stop when I leave the office. It follows me home, into the quiet moments when I'm cooking dinner or lying awake at night. I replay conversations, lab results, and subtle details that might mean something I missed. I wonder if I read enough, thought enough, or asked the right questions. There's always this whispering fear that my lack of attention could allow something bad to happen. I worry and worry and worry. Sometimes, the anxiety builds into a wave that feels like I'm choking, my chest tightens, my breath catches, and I'm overcome by a fear I rarely name aloud, that I'm not enough for this work.

It's humbling, this realization that no matter how much knowledge or experience I have, I can never silence that worry completely. My patients occupy space in my mind and heart long after the day ends. They are not just cases; they are people I care about, people whose lives intersect with mine in ways that often feel personal. I wake up some mornings thinking about the ones I wish I'd had more time to help, the ones whose stories stay with me.

***

Darren and Rosalyn were married for 58 years before he died. They raised three incredible children who grew into extraordinary adults. When I met Darren, I quickly realized he was an eternal optimist. His body was falling apart, yet that never stopped him. He had severe neuropathy and could no longer feel his feet. Still, he walked everywhere, steadily, with two walking sticks, eager to see and experience everything alongside Rosalyn.

When we first met, he told me about his cancer diagnosis. Ten years earlier, doctors had told him he had only a couple of years to live, that the cancer had already metastasized. But my patient, my friend, the eternal optimist with an infectious love for life, refused to accept that. He found a specialist across the country, flew there every six months for treatment, and lived nearly eight more years. In between appointments, he traveled, laughed, and lived fully with Rosalyn by his side.

Once, after returning from a trip out West, he showed me a photo of himself riding a massive horse. When he saw my eyes widen with surprise, he knew what I was wondering. How the hell did he get on that horse? He laughed in that deep, comforting way of his and said, "It took three big men to get me on and off that horse."

In the last year of his life, Darren was hospitalized several times. Each time, he bounced back, until, one day, he couldn't. I saw him in the ICU a few days before he passed. He was breathing heavily, with Rosalyn and one of their sons standing nearby, gazing at him with warmth and love. I held his hand and told him that if we took him off his breathing device, he likely wouldn't leave the hospital. If he worsened, he'd need to be intubated. He asked if there was anything else we could do. In preparation for his death, we talked about palliative care and hospice.

Through our discussions, I asked Darren about his death goals, and he stated that he didn't want to die in the hospital. I explained to him that most people don't want that either, but unfortunately, he was not stable enough to transfer home. I cried. He cried. And he understood. He told me he wasn't afraid of dying, only of leaving Rosalyn and their daughter behind.

I want to briefly acknowledge that, even though most people wish to die at home, the sad truth is that most do not. We are rarely prepared—logistically, emotionally, systemically—to make dying at home possible. And perhaps that is a kind of failure on our part. As a geriatrician, I am the physician most often entrusted to help patients prepare for this stage of life, and yet I had failed him.

Even in primary care, the system has changed so much that, despite being the physicians who walk with patients through every phase of life, we're given minutes for the living, and almost none for the dying. We manage medications, lab results, and insurance requirements, but not the quiet conversations that matter most—the ones about what it means to live and to die on one's own terms.

When I returned the next day, Darren had made his decision—he was ready. Over the following days, we transitioned him to hospice care, and he passed away peacefully. That weekend, I was home with my children while Jas was working in the ICU. The house felt unusually still, the kind of quiet that feels heavy, like it knows something you don't want to say aloud. I was waiting for Jas to come home so I could return to the hospital when my phone buzzed. It was a text from Jas: *Darren passed away peacefully*. I sat there for a long moment, staring at the message. Even when death is expected, it still feels like time pauses—one breath marking the end of a life, and another reminding you that your own continues.

I sat in silence, the same loud, familiar silence I have known too many times before. Then I sobbed. I cried for him, for Rosalyn, for their family, and for the love they shared. I cried because I would miss him, his stories, his laugh, his courage, and his unshakable zest for life.

Darren was the embodiment of adaptability, someone who refused to see his walking sticks as a disability, but rather as tools of independence, ways to move through the world on his own terms. He outlived the prediction by nearly a decade, and in the end, it wasn't the cancer.

After I stopped crying, I sat and wondered if there was something I could have done differently—some way to have given Darren just a little more time. When I get anxious or sad, when doubt begins to whisper and the worry sets in, I return to work. The anxiety eases, not because it disappears, but because I can act again. The discomfort becomes focus, and worry becomes problem-solving.

Maybe that's part of the balance I've learned to live with: accepting that worry and compassion coexist. Caring deeply will always carry a measure of unease. But it's that same discomfort that keeps me sharp, meaning attentive, not arrogant. Sharp, in the sense of staying present and aware, always questioning myself and learning from others.

There are physicians far more brilliant than I am—specialists whose depth of knowledge I depend on to give my patients the best care possible. Part of being a good doctor, I've come to realize, is knowing when to reach out, when to ask for help, and when to recognize that caring well is rarely a solo act.

***

When I first met my husband all those years ago, I was—and still am—captivated by him. In my mind's eye, I picture him walking into an ICU room during a code blue, emerging moments later with a sense of triumph—like a superhero stepping out of a whirlwind of fire and chaos, having just saved a patient's life. His chest is puffed out, his cape flowing behind him. Perhaps his emblem would be the Rod of Asclepius, the ancient staff with a single serpent coiled around it, the timeless symbol of healing. I can't help but giggle at the thought; it makes me feel like a teenage girl again.

And maybe part of why I see him this way is because of how my own mind works. It's always been a little twisted, a little too alive. I've had an overactive imagination for as long as I can remember. Someone will say something—an image, a word, a fleeting expression—and suddenly I'm somewhere else. It's as if I've slipped out of my body and stepped into a scene already unfolding. I can see the light, the setting, the emotion of it all. It plays out in my mind like a film I didn't know I was directing. I daydream vividly, almost cinematically. And this is the first time I've ever admitted that—at least as an adult.

But of course, I know Jas isn't a superhero. I've seen the nights when he comes home after impossible hours, his face drawn with exhaustion, his eyes distant. I know the moments when he feels he's failed—when a young person dies despite every effort, or when he has to look into a family's eyes and tell them their loved one is gone. Those are the nights when the weight of what he carries settles heavily on him, and even though he rarely says much, I can see it. I can feel it. It's a quiet worry that lives beneath the surface, the same way my own worry lives beneath mine.

And I have to admit, all this thinking sometimes makes me feel like a philosopher from ancient Greece—perhaps Plato or Socrates—contemplating the profound questions of patient care and the complexities of aging. It's a bit amusing, really, how I find myself lost in these reflections, as though I'm channeling the wisdom of the ancients. My thoughts rarely stay in one lane. They branch, collide, and spiral into unexpected places.

At work, it's become something of a running joke. Before

patients arrive, I'll call out across the hall, "I've been thinking," and from the other room, Stephanie, our medical assistant, will start laughing and say, "Oh boy, she's been thinking again." Everyone knows what that means—I've come up with a new idea, a new process, or some project that's going to create more work for all of us.

At home, it's no different. I'll say to Jas, "We should do something," and without missing a beat, he'll grin and say, "You mean *I* should." He's not wrong. One of my "we should" turned into removing a fireplace and replacing that same wall with a wall of windows so I could look out into the yard. Somehow, the things I imagine, Jas manages to make real.

The truth is, my mind rarely stops—and it's exhausting. For decades I have had to deal with ADHD and managing it has been a lifelong balancing act. The irony isn't lost on me that, as a physician with a bicuspid aortic valve, the very medications that might help me focus aren't ideal for my heart. So, I've had to find other ways to regulate my racing thoughts. The gym has become my therapy—the one place where everything slows down just enough for my mind to catch up with itself. I go early in the morning, when the world is still quiet. That first burst of dopamine steadies me, gives me clarity, and sets the tone for my day.

But self-awareness only gets me so far. I've learned that my enthusiasm, my tendency to leap before looking, can sometimes land me in trouble. I've signed contracts too quickly, made impulsive purchases, or jumped into new projects without thinking through the details. That's where the people around me come in—Kate, my business partner; Jas, my husband; Golnar, my sister and others who know me well. They help me see what my distracted mind sometimes misses. They catch the fine print I skip, ask the questions I forget to ask, and gently pull me back to earth when my excitement starts to outrun reason.

They are my grounding forces—the balance to my motion. They turn my restless energy into something tangible, something lasting. Without them, I'd be lost in the current of my own imagination, forever thinking, but never building.

***

Geriatricians are an interesting breed of doctors. As I've mentioned before, we're not exactly the most thrilling specialty, nor do we fit the typical mold of superheroes. Instead, we resemble ancient philosophers, thinkers who ponder the big questions of existence: gravity, space, time, and the continuum of before, present, and future. Our work often involves delving into these profound aspects of life, reflecting deeply on our patients' needs and conditions. Sometimes, I feel like I'm chasing my own tail, endlessly turning over thoughts and ideas in my quest to provide the best care. But I do it for my patients, the individuals I've had the pleasure to get to know and love deeply. In spending time with them, understanding their lives, and sharing their struggles and joys, I find a profound connection and affection.

Perhaps geriatricians were born to be geriatricians. From a young age, I found myself drawn to the company of elderly people, seeking out their presence and wisdom. There was a unique peace and strength that I drew from their stories and experiences. As a child, spending time with them felt natural and comforting, almost as if I was meant to be in their midst. Their strength and wisdom shaped my perspective on life, influencing my path into geriatrics. It's as though this affinity for the elderly was ingrained in me from the start, guiding me to a profession where I can continue to find meaning and fulfillment in their company.

In my mad scientist mechanic shop, it's like a scene from a Star Wars movie where the mechanic fixes anything and everything that is clunky and old. Picture me hammering away, clicking and clanking, trying to figure out what the hell is going on with each complex, malfunctioning machine, representing my patients' intricate conditions. I'm sweating under the pressure, knowing that I must repair what is wrong so the family members and loved ones can better understand and manage the situation. Just as a mechanic is attached to their tools and machines, so too am I deeply connected to my patients and their families. My role is not just about diagnosing and treating but also about helping families navigate the labyrinth of care, ensuring that they find clarity amidst the clunkiness and confusion of the medical world.

One example of the delicate balance between medical intervention and honoring patient wishes unfolded with a patient who had become more than just a case to me. She was in her early 80s, sharp, and had woven warmth into our lives with handmade blankets for my daughters. When the time came to discuss her goals of care, she was clear: she wanted comfort, not intervention and not to prolong her death. However, during an emergency endoscopy (an endoscopy is a procedure that lets doctors look inside the body with a thin, flexible camera to diagnose problems with clarity and minimal discomfort), her esophagus was tragically perforated, leading to an intubation that contradicted her wishes. I rushed to the ICU, where, despite my husband's heroic efforts to stabilize her, her condition worsened. And yes just another example of how my husband and I ended up caring for the same patient. Each day, as I walked in to see her, Lois would mouth her plea to turn off the machines.

I was so wrapped up in the urgency of the situation that I momentarily lost sight of her wishes, unable to fully grasp the gravity of our reality. My husband had to jolt me back into my role, explaining clearly and compassionately that we could do no more but honor her wishes. With tears in our eyes, her granddaughter and I faced the heart-wrenching decision to let Lois go. Sometimes even the most capable hands and the deepest philosophical reflections can't change certain outcomes. Sometimes, all we can do is adapt to the inevitability, embrace the limits of our control, and find solace in the love and respect we can still offer.

Medicine has indeed come a long way, transforming the landscape of patient care with remarkable advancements. We have the tools and technologies to patch up the most complex conditions, extend life, and provide temporary solutions to seemingly insurmountable problems. Yet, despite these incredible strides, there remains a finite boundary that we cannot cross. Each medical intervention, no matter how sophisticated, is bound by the reality of a beginning and an end. The art of medicine, therefore, is not just about extending life but about adapting to the natural course of existence. We must recognize and respect these limits, understanding that our role is to guide our patients through the complexities of their conditions with compassion and dignity. In the face of this finite nature, adapting becomes not just a necessity but a profound act of respect for the cycles of life and the journey we all must eventually undertake.

Even though I've learned about adaptation not only through my own life but also through my patients, I believe we all have countless opportunities to study adaptation in motion, through the people we care for, the loved ones we observe, and the stories shared by those who have lived long enough to have reinvented themselves many times over. Listening to our elders describe how they learned to live again after loss or disease is like being handed a map of human resilience. They remind us that life, in its simplest form, is an ongoing lesson in letting go and beginning again.

My father is one of my greatest teachers in this. He once dreamed of becoming an engineer, building bridges and designing cities, but life had other plans. Circumstances beyond his control altered his path, forcing him to trade his ambitions for the demands of survival in a new country, a new language, and an unfamiliar culture. His journey was defined by financial strain, relentless work, and the quiet, persistent effort to make ends meet. Yet he never saw his perseverance as resilience, to him, it was simply what had to be done.

There were times when that struggle took a toll. I remember periods of tension and sadness in our home, moments when my father seemed weighed down by disappointment and mental exhaustion. He had come from a life of stability and respect to one of uncertainty, and that transformation broke something inside him for a time. As a child, I didn't understand. I felt anger, confusion, and even resentment. But as I grew older, I began to see that much of what I had mistaken for weakness was actually pain, the kind that comes from being forced to rebuild a life from the ground up.

Now, as an adult, I see him differently. I see a man who

adapted in the only ways he could, who kept moving forward even when the road disappeared beneath his feet. I've come to realize that my anger was never truly justified. It was born from not yet understanding what survival looks like. Life humbles all of us. In the end, humanity is simply the act of trying to survive, to keep going despite the ache of what we've lost. My father's quiet endurance taught me that adaptability isn't always graceful or courageous; sometimes it's just the strength to keep breathing, one day at a time.

Similarly, my mother's story is one of profound adaptability. She and my father navigated the challenges of starting anew in a different country, facing frequent financial difficulties and personal conflicts. Despite their hardships, they remained committed to supporting our education and well-being. They didn't see their efforts as acts of resilience, but looking back, it's clear that their ability to persevere and adapt in the face of adversity was indeed a powerful testament to their strength. Their legacy of resilience, though unrecognized by them at the time, continues to guide me, reinforcing that no matter the challenges, there's always a path forward if we remain open to change.

My uncle's life is a testament to extraordinary strength and adaptability. His journey began with a dramatic episode during the Iranian revolution when he was shot while aiding young Iranians in their escape. Despite his grave injury, he managed to board a plane, revealing his wound only after they had cleared Iranian airspace. The flight attendant, upon seeing his condition, fainted, prompting an emergency landing in Turkey where he underwent life-saving surgery.

This harrowing experience was just the beginning of a life

marked by remarkable adaptability. Over the years, he survived a ruptured aneurysm, cancer, a heart attack, and now, more cancer that has spread extensively. Through each challenge, he has adapted to new limitations with a steadfast smile and enduring purpose. His story is also one of global adventure, he lived across various countries, learned seven languages, and interacted with a diverse array of people. An iconic moment in his life was carrying the torch at the 2002 Salt Lake City Olympics, symbolizing his journey of a life well lived.

His personal life reflects a deep and abiding love. His wife, a physician with her own challenges, has shared this journey with him, adapting and supporting each other through life's ups and downs. Their bond and her unwavering support highlight the strength found in mutual adaptation and love. My uncle's ability to embrace change and maintain a positive outlook, even in the face of daunting obstacles, serves as a profound lesson in the power of resilience and the beauty of living life fully despite its adversities.

In many ways, my life had been preparing me from a young age for the concept of adapting to change, a lesson that was deeply reinforced by my patients and the experiences that shaped me. The loss of James was a pain that can never be fully embraced, yet as humans, we learn to adapt, to continue moving forward even in the face of unimaginable loss. I've witnessed this resilience among my female colleagues, mothers, doctors, and wives who continue to persevere despite losing children or spouses and enduring countless hardships.

This is a tribute to the women in medicine, and especially to my incredible practice partner, Dr. Kathleen Blaney (Kate), who seems to weave her way through the unexpected with effortless grace. She is tall, with long, flowing red hair that always catches the light just right, and eyes so strikingly blue they almost seem translucent. There's a clarity in them that makes you feel as though you can see straight into her soul—eyes that seem to perceive the world not just as it is, but as it could be. When you see her photo, it looks like a professional headshot; she could easily pass for a model.

Her strength and grace remind me that resilience doesn't always roar. Sometimes it's quiet, poised, and steady—the kind that endures without demanding attention. And that, too, is a form of adaptation.

I've always joked that I'm her opposite: short, dark-haired, a bit of a whirlwind. But I've learned to stay close to people like Kate because she brings a calmness that steadies me. She sees sides of situations I might miss and approaches challenges with a kind of quiet wisdom that I deeply admire. She is calm where I'm kinetic, deliberate where I'm instinctive. I suppose we're both centered in our own ways—hers like still water, mine more like fire—and somewhere in that balance, we've found a rhythm that works. That balance has made us successful together, not because we're the same, but because we've learned to trust and lean into each other's strengths.

***

One of the most profound examples of resilience and adaptation I've witnessed involved Frank, a patient living with Parkinson's disease. When I first met him, he had been living with the diagnosis for more than fifteen years. He still walked with a cane then, determined to maintain his independence and his sense of dignity. But over time, Parkinson's began to take more from him. The cane gave way to a walker, and eventually, the walker to a wheelchair. His movements slowed, his muscles stiffened, and when he could no longer swallow safely, a feeding tube became his lifeline.

Throughout this long decline, Elaine, his wife of more than fifty years, stood by his side with a steadiness that was both inspiring and heartbreaking. With each new challenge, she found a way to adapt. She rearranged their home, learned how to manage the feeding tube, and made sure he had everything he needed to preserve even the smallest comforts of daily life.

As Frank began to sleep more, Elaine and I often found ourselves talking quietly in her living room while he rested nearby. She always had a pot of fresh coffee brewing, and those afternoons became moments of unexpected connection. Over time, our conversations drifted from his medical care to her life, the early years of their marriage, the trips they took, and how her world had slowly come to revolve entirely around him. When I asked about her family, she smiled softly and said that Frank was really all she had. I found myself thinking often about what would happen when he was gone, though I never said it out loud.

Despite his physical decline, Frank remained mentally sharp and fully present. He didn't let his worsening condition extinguish his spirit; instead, he adapted to each new limitation with quiet determination. Elaine matched that spirit in her own way, never giving up, never allowing despair to eclipse the deep love that anchored them both. Their story reminded me that resilience isn't about standing firm against hardship; it's about learning to bend without breaking, to find new ways of being when old ones fade away. Just like Darren, Frank and Elaine didn't see change as something to fight, but as something to walk alongside, bending when they needed to, holding firm when it mattered most.

In the end, when it became clear that even the feeding tube could no longer offer Frank comfort or connection with the world, I was called to their home. Elaine, ever the vigilant caregiver, had reached a place of quiet acceptance, ready to shift her focus from prolonging life to preserving peace. With a gentle nod from Frank and Elaine's unwavering support, I removed the feeding tube, honoring his wish for a dignified and natural end.

Afterward, I hugged them both, my chest heavy with the weight of love and loss. I couldn't help but marvel at the quiet strength they had shown, adapting to every twist and turn that Parkinson's had thrown their way. Together, they had embraced change not as tragedy, but as a final act of devotion. In their grace, I saw what it truly means to live, and to let go, with love.

This ability to adapt in the face of profound loss is something I've witnessed time and time again, like in the story of another patient. Gayle's story is a beautiful example of love, resilience, and adaptation. He was an accomplished engineer who may have had a hand in the development of vancomycin, a significant contribution to medicine. But beyond his professional achievements, it was his deep love for his wife that truly defined his life. He often reminisced about their time together in Vienna, sharing tales of her adventurous spirit, like when she tried to smuggle artwork while he was at work. He spoke fondly of their walks through the streets of Vienna, always emphasizing her beauty and how much he depended on her emotionally.

When I met Gayle, he had recently moved to a retirement

community, trying to find his way after her sudden passing from leukemia. Despite the profound loss, he found a way to adapt. He picked up pickleball, a sport that was just gaining popularity at the time, and introduced it to the community. Through this new activity, he made friends and embraced his new surroundings. Like my Parkinson's patient, Gayle understood that adapting to change requires a willingness to see life in a different light, to remain flexible, and to find new ways to connect with the world around him. Even in the face of such a devastating loss, Gayle found ways to move forward, honoring the memory of his wife while continuing to live a meaningful life.

My patients have taught me that true happiness often depends on our ability to adapt in the face of adversity. This insight resonates deeply with the themes in *The Happiness Hypothesis* by Jonathan Haidt, which explores how our internal mindset shapes our well-being more than external circumstances. Haidt emphasizes that happiness is less about avoiding hardship and more about how we respond to it, how we find meaning in what remains when so much has been taken away.

I've seen this truth reflected in patients like Frank, who, even as Parkinson's disease steadily stole his physical abilities, continued to live with grace and engagement, supported every step of the way by his devoted wife, Elaine. Their strength showed me that dignity is not lost in decline; it is sustained through love, patience, and acceptance. I've also seen it in Darren, the eternal optimist who faced terminal cancer with humor and wonder, defying every prediction and living years beyond what anyone thought possible. He refused to let fear or illness define his days, choosing instead to see beauty and meaning in the time he still had. Both men taught me that resilience and adaptation are not passive forms of endurance, they are active, deliberate expressions of the human spirit.

And then there is Gayle, who, after losing his wife to leukemia, found a way to begin again. He built new routines, picked up pickleball, and slowly created a vibrant community around him. His ability to shift perspective and find joy in small, everyday moments mirrors Haidt's idea that reframing challenges can foster lasting fulfillment.

Together, their stories remind me that happiness isn't about escaping pain or loss, it's about the courage to keep engaging with life, to keep adapting, and to keep finding meaning in the spaces that change leaves behind. And though I first encountered these ideas while reading *The Happiness Hypothesis*, I realize now that I didn't need a book to teach me. The real lessons came from spending time with these incredible people, the ones who showed me, through their quiet strength and resilience, what it truly means to live well, to love deeply, and to adapt with grace.

In contrast, patients like Helen, who remained rigid, isolated, and unable to accept new approaches, struggled far more profoundly. Helen had prepared her home for disability long before she actually became disabled. When I spoke with one of her family members, they told me they were surprised when she requested a motorized wheelchair even though she could still walk. It was as if she was preparing for decline before it arrived, building her life around an expectation of limitation rather than possibility.

Helen refused physical therapy because, she said, it hurt too much. She declined medications that could have helped manage her pain and stiffness, convinced their side effects would only make things worse. Over time, her fear of discomfort and her mistrust of others began to consume her. She often spoke as if the world was conspiring against her, her ex-husband, her nurses, her doctors, and I sometimes wondered if she felt the same way about me. I knew I couldn't change her perspective, but I could listen and continue to show up, hoping that consistency itself might offer a small measure of comfort.

Sadly, the negativity that surrounded her gradually became the environment she lived in. Her physical decline accelerated, her strength faded, and the very independence she had feared losing slipped away. She became fully reliant on her motorized wheelchair, and eventually, even that wasn't enough. She could no longer transfer without help and needed assistance with the simplest daily tasks, brushing her hair, toileting, dressing. It was heartbreaking to watch someone's world become so small, not solely because of disease, but because of fear's power to limit possibility.

Helen's story reinforces Haidt's point that resistance to change can erode happiness, while openness and flexibility are essential to resilience. Her life became a reminder that adaptation is not just a physical act; it's an emotional and spiritual one.

In stark contrast, another patient, Barb, faced similar physical challenges but approached her situation with a different mindset. Despite her disabilities, Barb actively sought out specialists to improve her health and remained open to new approaches when something wasn't working. She went to dinner with friends, traveled, and pursued hobbies that kept her engaged with life. Her willingness to adapt, to try again, and to find meaning in connection allowed her to experience joy even in the face of hardship.

This contrast underscores Haidt's notion that a sense of purpose and the ability to adapt are crucial for enduring happiness, even in the face of significant adversity. Helen prepared for decline and lived within its walls. Barb prepared for life and continued to live within its vastness.

I've encountered a wide range of attitudes towards aging and health in my patients, each revealing unique perspectives on life and its challenges. One patient, an 88-year-old woman, stood out for her remarkable outlook. Despite her age and declining health, she maintained an enthusiastic spirit. She took great joy in redecorating her entire house, frequently updating her decor to stay current with modern trends. Each visit, we would discuss paint colors, new furniture, and landscaping ideas. Her passion for decorating was not merely a hobby; it was a testament to her refusal to accept a diminished role in her own life. She continued to live with a vibrant sense of purpose and maintained a forward-looking attitude, seeing her home as a reflection of her ongoing engagement with the world.

In contrast, I've encountered patients who, facing similar challenges, felt a sense of resignation. Some would say things like, "I'm going to die anyway; why should I spend money on this?" or "What's the point of doing anything?" Their outlook was often marked by a sense of futility and a reluctance to invest in their present circumstances. This stark difference in attitude underscores how critical it is to maintain a sense of purpose and engagement, regardless of age or health status. The patient who continued to decorate her home with enthusiasm demonstrated how a positive attitude and an active involvement in life can profoundly impact one's overall sense of well-being and fulfillment.

These experiences highlight the profound impact of perspective on aging. While some may feel resigned to the inevitability of decline, others, like my decorating patient, find joy and purpose in every aspect of their lives, illustrating that engagement and a forward-thinking attitude can sustain happiness and vitality well into old age.

As I reflect on the diverse experiences and attitudes of my patients, I realize how profoundly they have shaped my own perspective on aging and life. Observing their resilience, adaptability, and zest for life has provided me insights into which attitudes truly resonate and which I aspire to embody as I grow older. The contrasts between those who embrace life's challenges with optimism and those who resign themselves to inevitability have illuminated the paths I wish to follow.

In the spirit of the "mad scientist" I've often embraced, a figure driven by curiosity, exploration, and the quest for understanding, I've come to see that our interactions with our elders offer the ultimate laboratory of human experience. By learning from their stories, their methods of adaptation, and their ways of accepting and embracing life, we gain profound wisdom about what it means to truly live. This journey has underscored a crucial truth: we must actively engage with and learn from those who have traversed the long path of life before us. It is through this engagement that we discover the most meaningful ways to navigate our own paths, ensuring that we, too, can face the future with the same spirit of resilience and curiosity that our elders so admirably display.

Chapter 9

Learning from Loss

I lost you, and I grieve knowing that I will never touch your face again. Yet, in the memories we shared, I find peace and comfort. You taught me about living, about embracing this world, and it is through these lessons that I carry your spirit forward.

Loss is a strange word to use when someone dies, yet it's a word we often turn to. We know where they are, they are dead. They are dead and we have to move forward; they are dead, not lost. The word *loss* perhaps serves to soften the blow, like the loss of self, the loss of an object, the loss of a job, the loss of a marriage, or the loss of a child growing up and moving away. Most losses are temporary in nature; we can often come to a place of finding or recovery. But the death of a loved one- that is permanent. And yet we don't tell a grieving person, "I am sorry for your dead," we say, "I am sorry for your loss."

We don't say *dead* because the word feels too final, too violent, too real. *Loss* allows for softness; it gives grief edges we can hold without cutting ourselves. It leaves room for memory, for the possibility that love still exists somewhere, even if the person does not. Maybe that's why we cling to the word, because *loss* implies something misplaced, not entirely gone. It keeps the door cracked open, allowing us to imagine that in some way, shape, or form, we might still find them again.

When my patients die, I often think about that word. Loss. What exactly was lost? The person, of course, but also the shared laughter, the conversations, the future that would have unfolded if time had allowed. The loss extends beyond the individual; it ripples through the spaces they once filled, the empty chair, the voicemail that still plays, the scent left behind on a shirt. Perhaps we say *loss* because grief isn't just about death, it's about absence. It's about learning to live in the hollow places where love used to dwell.

Over the years, my thoughts about death have shifted. I am certain they will continue to shift. We are born, we live, and we die, and somewhere in between, we travel through this brief existence trying to make sense of what it all means. From the earth we came, and to the earth, we return. The body knows this cycle even if the mind resists it. I often wonder: do we truly go somewhere, to heaven, to another realm, to a place beyond our understanding, or do we somehow stay? Do we linger in the energy we've left behind, in the memories and love that still ripple through others? I don't have the answers, but I've come to accept that perhaps understanding isn't the point. Maybe death isn't meant to be solved, only softened through meaning.

Perhaps the loss of someone who has died is tied to our beliefs, beliefs that provide us with a framework to understand and cope with death. In Buddhism, the loss may be seen as part of the cycle of rebirth, an individual's journey from one life to another, with death as a transition rather than an end. In Christianity and Islam, death is often viewed as a passage to an eternal afterlife, with heaven as the ultimate destination for those who have lived in accordance with their faith. This belief in an afterlife offers solace, suggesting that the deceased are not truly lost but have moved on to a place of peace.

In Hinduism, the concept of reincarnation plays a central role. The soul is believed to be eternal, passing through a continuous cycle of birth, death, and rebirth, guided by karma. Each life becomes a chapter in a much larger story, one that extends far beyond what we can see or understand. The loss, then, is only of the physical form; the essence of the person continues to exist, to learn, to evolve. Death, in this view, is not an ending but a transformation, a return to something larger than oneself.

I often think of this when sitting with families who are grieving. There is always a sense that something intangible remains, the warmth of a hand once held, the familiar way a laugh echoes in memory, the love that lingers in the air even after the person is gone. Perhaps these are small glimpses of that spiritual continuity, the ways in which the soul, or whatever word we choose to give it, keeps weaving itself into the lives of those left behind.

Across many faiths, loss is interpreted through the lens of

continuity rather than absence. Whether through reincarnation, heaven, or the enduring energy of love, there is a shared human hope that death is not destruction but transition. And maybe that hope itself, the belief that life somehow continues, is what allows us to keep living after loss.

Likewise, in Judaism, the focus turns toward remembrance. Judaism often emphasizes the importance of remembering the deceased, with traditions that keep their memory alive through rituals, prayers, and the recitation of their names. The *Kaddish*, for instance, is not a prayer for the dead but a declaration of life, an affirmation of faith even in the face of grief. In this way, loss is acknowledged openly, yet the focus shifts toward honoring the life that was lived and the legacy left behind. Memory becomes sacred work. It transforms grief into something active, allowing those who mourn to continue loving through remembrance.

Similarly, many Indigenous belief systems view death not as separation but as a return, a homecoming to the earth, or a reunion with ancestors. The individual becomes part of the natural world again, woven back into the soil, the wind, the water, and the stories passed from one generation to the next. There is a beautiful symmetry in that idea: the understanding that we come from the earth, and to it we return, not as disappearance but as transformation. As a physician, I see all of these beliefs expressed in the quiet moments after death — in the way families pray, hold a hand, or simply sit in silence. Each gesture, no matter the faith, seems to whisper the same truth: love doesn't end here.

Across these traditions, there's a common thread: the belief that death does not erase existence but reshapes it. Whether through ritual, remembrance, or the quiet knowing that we rejoin something greater than ourselves, these beliefs offer comfort. They remind us that even when a body is gone, the connection remains, living on in prayer, in the rhythm of the earth, and in the hearts of those who remember.

Across different religions and cultures, the concept of loss is deeply intertwined with beliefs about what happens after death. These beliefs shape how we mourn, how we honor those who have passed, and how we find meaning in their absence. For some, death marks a doorway to another existence; for others, it is a merging back into the fabric of the universe, a return to the rhythm of creation itself. Whether the language is spiritual, poetic, or rooted in ritual, each belief system offers a path toward understanding, a way to make sense of the unbearable.

In my years of caring for patients and their families, I've come to see that belief, in whatever form it takes, serves as a bridge between the living and the dead. It allows us to imagine our loved ones not as vanished, but as continuing on in some altered state, as energy, as memory, as spirit, as love. It helps the living adapt, providing structure to grief when the world feels unstructured. Loss, then, is not only about physical absence; it becomes part of a larger spiritual journey, one that gives both the living and the departed a way to remain connected in realms beyond the tangible world.

And maybe that is the quiet mercy of belief. It does not erase pain or replace the person we've lost, but it helps us survive them. It gives us a way to keep reaching for meaning, to keep loving across the distance between here and whatever lies beyond.

This is likely why we use the word *loss*: because, rooted in these beliefs, when someone dear to us passes, we cling to the hope of reunion. We hold on to the possibility that they will be found again in some form, whether through spiritual beliefs, memories, or legacies. The word *loss* gives us permission to imagine continuity, that love endures even when the body does not, that something remains to be found when so much has been taken. In this way, the concept of loss becomes more bearable when framed within the possibility of future connection.

As a physician who works at the intersection of life and death, I've learned that understanding loss requires more than clinical knowledge. It demands empathy for the unseen. To truly care for a dying person, I must understand the person *behind* the diagnosis, the web of relationships that hold them, and the beliefs that shape how they and their loved ones will experience parting. Every family grieves differently; every room holds its own sacred rhythm of silence, ritual, and remembrance.

It is not my place to interpret loss for them. My responsibility is to step quietly into their circle, to learn their language of mourning and hope, and to honor it. To do otherwise would be to intrude on something holy. When I meet people where they are, whether that means praying with them, sitting in silence, or simply holding a hand, I am reminded that healing isn't always about curing. Sometimes it's about presence, about bearing witness to love as it transforms from something visible to something eternal.

When I first establish care with a patient, I am often met with looks of surprise when I ask about the spiritual or cultural beliefs that may influence their care. These questions sometimes catch people off guard, yet they are as essential as any discussion about medications or treatment plans. They reveal how a person understands suffering, hope, and death, truths that no lab result can measure. These beliefs, though not my own, are ones I must uphold and honor. They are beliefs I will defend, even when they differ from what I personally understand or believe to be true.

As a physician privileged to accompany my patients through their journey of life and death, I've learned that caring requires flexibility, not just in practice, but in spirit, and that lesson extends far beyond medicine. It's about meeting people where they are, in whatever form their pain, hope, or belief takes. Whether at a bedside, in a friendship, or within a family, compassion demands that we bend before we break, that we listen before we act.

I have prayed with patients whose faith was foreign to me. Bowed with families before their loved one's body, and washed the body of a patient alongside their family to honor them after death. In those moments, I did not act as their doctor but as a fellow human being, a witness to love and loss expressed in its purest form. Through it all, I have been profoundly grateful to be invited into these sacred spaces, places where faith, love, and mortality intersect.

To be accepted in moments of such vulnerability is a privilege I do not take lightly. Each time, I am reminded that medicine is not just a science of the body but a ministry of presence. It asks us to show up, to listen, to honor the unseen, and to remember that every act of compassion, however small, is a way of saying: *I see you, I stand with you, and I will help carry the weight of this loss.*

***

Betty was a deeply valued patient I met during my third year of residency in family medicine. At that point, I had begun to push the boundaries of conventional practice by making house calls and forming more personal connections with my patients. While my attendings were aware of my unconventional methods, my approach was evolving. I was no longer just a doctor; I was becoming part of their lives, their extended family. One night, while I was the resident on call, the emergency room asked me to admit Betty, who was in her sixties. Her condition was severe; she had been living with untreated cancer that had grotesquely disfigured her face. This experience profoundly impacted me, as it highlighted the significance of not just providing medical care but also offering compassion and emotional support, thereby deepening my commitment to truly understanding and connecting with my patients.

Over the following days, after Betty was admitted to the hospital, I got to know her and her family much better. Her husband, whom I'll refer to as Jim, was unwavering in his support. He stayed by her side every day, his hands resting on the edge of her bed, his voice soft but steady as he tried to understand what had gone wrong. He couldn't comprehend why she had waited so long to seek help.

When I spoke with Betty, she admitted that fear had kept her away, fear of doctors, hospitals, and what she imagined awaited her once she stepped inside one. She told me about past experiences where she felt unheard or dismissed, times when she left an office feeling smaller than when she walked in. Her hesitation was not rooted in denial but in self-protection. Her fear wasn't of medicine itself but of not being seen.

That realization shifted something in me. I understood

that what may seem trivial or routine to one person can feel overwhelming to another, depending on what they've endured. In medicine, I had to learn to approach people gently, with awareness that my words or expressions could either build trust or quietly fracture it. But this truth reaches far beyond medicine. It exists in every human interaction, in how we speak to our partners, raise our children, comfort a friend, or meet a stranger in pain. The energy we bring into an encounter, our tone, our patience, our openness, determines whether people lean toward us or away from us.

Betty's fear was a mirror, reflecting how easily misunderstanding can harden into mistrust. Had her earlier encounters been different, had she felt safe, heard, and respected, she might have sought help long before her illness worsened. It made me realize that every exchange carries the potential to heal or to wound, to open someone's heart or to close it. And that responsibility belongs to all of us, not just to those in medicine.

In the end, empathy isn't a professional skill; it's a way of being in the world. It's how we communicate to others, *"You are safe here. I see you."* Whether in a hospital room, at a dinner table, or in the quiet moments between friends, empathy is what transforms interaction into connection, and connection, into healing.

I arranged for an oncology consult, and our oncologist, who was exceptional, took over Betty's care. Her type of cancer, while generally rare in metastasizing because people usually address it early, had unfortunately spread extensively. Betty required surgical intervention, which further disfigured her face, followed by chemotherapy. Eventually, she was told she was cancer-free. Despite no longer being officially her doctor, I continued to stay in touch with Betty and Jim over the following months. Betty would call me when she was scared, and Jim reached out with questions and concerns. Despite ongoing visits to oncology and their primary care doctor, Betty's health continued to decline. She lost more weight, and although she had been declared cancer-free, her condition did not improve.

This experience was a humbling reminder of the limits of our medical knowledge. There are times when, despite our best efforts, we cannot fully understand or fix certain things, and sometimes, we must confront the painful reality that not all problems have solutions.

One day, as I was heading home after work, Jim called me in a state of panic, informing me that Betty was unresponsive. He was unsure of what to do and had reached out to the oncologist, who advised him to bring her to the hospital. However, given Betty's frailty, I feared she might not survive the trip. I spent about ten minutes on the phone with Jim, discussing Betty's wishes, her condition over the past few days, and letting him know I was on my way. Simultaneously, the oncologist called me, suggesting that, given my close relationship with the family, I should instruct them to go to the hospital. I conveyed to the oncologist that I believed Betty was nearing the end of her life. When I arrived at her home about fifteen minutes later, I found that Betty had already passed away. Jim told me she had died about five minutes after our phone conversation. I called the oncologist back to inform him of the news- which was a shock. Jim welcomed me inside, and we shared a heartfelt hug. I approached Betty's still-warm body, said my goodbyes, and cried as I embraced her. Jim then introduced me to the family, and we spent the next couple of hours together. Jim explained that in their family tradition, the women closest to Betty would wash and prepare her body before the funeral home arrived. They invited me to stay and participate in this deeply personal ritual. I was profoundly touched and honored to be included in such an intimate moment, marking the end of Betty's journey and the beginning of her family's farewell.

My time with Betty and Jim had left a lasting impact on me. Betty's final days, surrounded by the warmth of her family, reminded me of the profound connections we form with our patients and their loved ones. It was a powerful testament to the strength of human relationships and the importance of compassion in the face of loss.

In the years following my experience with Betty and Jim, another deeply personal and challenging moment arose. One evening, as I was heading home after a long shift, I called Mr. Walsh to discuss his father's condition. This was one of the few times I remember every word exchanged. Our conversation still echoes in my mind,

"Hello, is this Mr. Walsh?" I asked as the man picked up his phone.
"Yes, it is. Who is this?" he replied.
"Sir, this is Dr. Sharafsaleh at the hospital. I'm a geriatrician who was asked to consult on your father's case, and I have some updates."
"Oh, thank you, doctor," he said.
I braced myself, knowing I was about to deliver difficult news. Before I even began, he had thanked me.

"Mr. Walsh, your father has not been doing very well. Over the last three days, he has not been participating in physical therapy. The nursing staff have had difficulty waking him. And this morning the nurse reported he started coughing after trying to give him a few drops of water." I took a breath and continued. "The medical team asked me to weigh in. I know your father from his recent admission about a month ago after his hip fracture." I paused, then added, "He is not doing well, sir. I wanted to discuss focusing on comfort care rather than continued measures to keep him alive." I finally said it: "Mr. Walsh, I think your father is dying." Then I remained silent.

"Doctor, can you explain what has been going on and why you think my father is dying?" he asked.

I began explaining to Mr. Walsh that the recent complications were overwhelming for his father. His 95-year-old father had severe dementia, a recent hip fracture, and now a COVID infection, which had led to delirium. "Doctor, what is delirium?" Mr. Walsh asked.

I explained that delirium is an acute confusional state, distinct from dementia, and that his father's severe dementia, physical debility, age, recent infection, and current environment contributed to it. I also referred him to my blog, GeriAcademy.com, where he could learn more about delirium.

Delirium can be frightening to witness. I was accustomed to seeing it and had grown less reactive than family members, who often found it alarming to see their loved ones yelling, hallucinating, or staring blankly. For Mr. Walsh, who couldn't see his father, it was especially confusing.

"Doctor, who did you say you were again?" Mr. Walsh asked after the heavy news. I reintroduced myself, explaining that I ran the palliative care service line at the hospital and that the hospitalist had asked me to weigh in.

"Doctor, what does my father's hip fracture have to do with this?" he inquired.

I explained that up to 20% of older adults who have a hip fracture die within the first year, and about half lose their independence. His father's severe dementia likely contributed to his inability to follow directions and participate in physical therapy, which led to further debility and weakened his immune system, causing more complications. I could visualize the snowball effect, growing larger and unstoppable.

"Mr. Walsh, I suspect your father has days to weeks to live. It's time to consider hospice and focus on his comfort," I said.

"I understand, doctor. Thank you for explaining that to me," he replied.

I continued to outline the next steps, focusing on comfort measures like keeping his father's mouth moist, administering medications for respiratory distress and pain. I asked if he had any questions.

"No, doctor. Thank you. You did that so effortlessly," he said.

"Effortlessly?" I asked.

"Yes, doctor. The way you told me my father was dying was so effortless, like you do that all the time. I would hate to have your job," he said. "How do you do your job?"

No one had ever said that to me before. I was taken aback. I had heard variations of "I could never do what you do," but this was different. I told Mr. Walsh the truth: it was never easy to deliver such news. I could only imagine how he must have felt and that I would deal with my emotions later. I offered him my cell phone number for any further questions.

Mr. Walsh thanked me, and I assured him I would coordinate with the social worker and primary medical team before ending the call.

Throughout our conversation, I kept my voice soft and made an effort to be compassionate and understanding. Regardless of age, every patient's life, death, and everything in between matters deeply.

Experiences like those with Betty and Mr. Walsh have been pivotal throughout my career. Each story and interaction has played a significant role in shaping who I am both as a physician and as a person. What stood out about Betty was the contrast between my youthful inexperience and the depth of the situation. In Mr. Walsh's case, it was his observation, years later, of how I discussed death with what seemed like effortless ease. Although these moments occurred at different times, they both illustrate how medicine and human interactions profoundly transform us. The experiences of my patients weave into my own journey, continuously influencing my growth and the person I am becoming.

***

When I look back on these moments, I realize that loss is not merely an ending but a profound teacher. Each experience of loss, whether personal or witnessed in others, has revealed something essential about the fragility of life and the resilience of the human spirit. Through grief and the quiet ache that follows it, we come to understand empathy in its truest form—not as pity, but as shared humanity. We learn that sorrow and love are intertwined, that meaning often emerges from within pain itself.

These lessons aren't theoretical or abstract; they are lived truths that shape how we move through the world and how we hold space for others in their suffering.

The stories of people like Betty, Mr. Walsh, and so many others continue to echo these truths back to me. Their lives remind me of the wisdom I've drawn from my patients and elders, those who have weathered the storms of time with grace, humor, and humility. Even as their bodies grew frail, their spirits carried the quiet authority of experience. They have endured loss upon loss, of health, independence, loved ones, yet still found reasons to hope, to laugh, to keep living. In them, I see the purest form of endurance: not defiance against change, but acceptance of it. Their ability to keep moving forward, to adapt again stands as a testament to the boundless strength of the human spirit.

As I delve into books on habit, strength, loss, influence, adversity, and triumph, I find that my patients, my elderly friends, and my parents have already imparted those lessons to me. Through spending time with them and truly listening to their stories, I have absorbed these teachings in the most authentic and profound way. Their lived experiences have provided me with a deeper understanding of these concepts, making the wisdom of their lives a living testament to the lessons I continue to learn.

***

In the midst of the profound sadness that enveloped me after losing my son, James, my husband gently reminded me of the strength and wisdom of my mother-in-law, Debbie. I cherish her deeply and hold her close to my heart, much like I would my own mother. Debbie had experienced her own immense loss when her daughter, Heather, tragically passed away in a car accident at a very young age. Despite the unimaginable heartache, she found a way to keep moving forward, one breath, one moment, one day at a time. She didn't have the luxury of falling apart completely. She had two other children who needed her, and somehow, she found the strength to keep showing up for them. Over the years, she has carried her grief with grace, transforming it into compassion and quiet wisdom.

I see that same strength mirrored in my father-in-law. Watching him play with my daughters, hearing his laughter fill the room, I sometimes think about all that exists beneath that warmth, the memories, the ache, the loss that time never fully mends. He has moved forward, building a beautiful life filled with love, joy, and family, yet I know there isn't a single day that passes when he doesn't think of Heather. Just as there isn't a day that passes when I don't think of James.

Their ability to live with both presence and absence, to hold joy in one hand and grief in the other, has taught me something profound about endurance. Grief never truly leaves us; it simply learns to live alongside the love that remains. Watching them, I've come to understand that healing isn't about forgetting, but about remembering differently, finding ways to let love take new shape, even after loss has rearranged everything we once knew.

Talking with Debbie, I am continually inspired by her ability to see the beauty in the world. She always has a smile on her face and manages to find the silver linings, even in adversity. Her perspective, shaped by her own experiences of loss and perseverance, has been a guiding light for me, reminding me that even in the darkest times, there is hope and strength to be found.

***

    Loss is an intrinsic part of our existence, shaping our lives in profound ways. It is through experiencing loss that we learn to truly appreciate the depth of love, the richness of our lives, and the moments in between that define us. Without loss, we might miss the true value of our joys and triumphs. Each loss teaches us about resilience, guiding us to weave new paths toward our own survival. These moments of pain and reflection deepen our understanding of what it means to live fully, to embrace love, and to navigate the journey with newfound strength and appreciation. In the tapestry of life, love, and the in-between, it is through the threads of loss that we learn not only how to endure, but how to love more deeply.

Chapter 10

Relevance

You are relevant, from the first breath you take until the moment you leave this earth. And even after you go, you remain a part of the lives you've touched, the lessons you've taught, the love you gave. That is relevance. Not the title or the productivity, but the presence — the imprint we leave behind.

"The ego identifies with form. It is the 'I am this'—doctor, parent, professional. When the form changes, the ego feels threatened. But the true self is formless presence."
—Eckhart Tolle, *The Power of Now*

My dear patient, whom I will refer to as Dan, was about five-foot-eight, though that day he seemed smaller, almost my height, and I'm only five-one. His body carried the swelling that heart failure brings, a heaviness that pulled him downward, as if gravity itself had become cruel. His skin had taken on a yellow hue, his eyes ringed with fatigue, his breathing shallow and effortful. When he walked into my exam room, each step was deliberate, his hands gripping the walker with quiet desperation

"I no longer feel relevant," he said softly. The words came out like an exhale, heavy and fragile, as though they had been waiting inside him for too long.

What normally takes seconds- the few steps from the door to the chair- took him nearly a full minute. I watched a man who had once been brisk, decisive, commanding, now winded, trembling, unsure. His mind was still sharp, but his body betrayed him. He had sent a text message earlier: *Weak. Dizzy. Something's not right.* And I could see it immediately, something was slipping.

So many things were going wrong at once. I was racing, ordering tests, bloodwork, imaging, talking to specialists, trying to hold all the pieces together. But beneath the urgency, I felt an ache I rarely admitted, the fear that I might not be able to fix this. That this was one of those moments when medicine could no longer rewrite the ending. I was scared. Dan was scared. And Clara, his lovely wife, shared in our fear.

But what struck me most wasn't just the illness; it was what he said. *"I no longer feel relevant."* The words lingered in the room like a confession, like the quiet realization that the world moves on even when we can't. His statement was not only about disease; it was about identity, about the loss of place and purpose when the body starts to fail. In that moment, I realized that relevance, that deep sense of being needed, useful, and seen, is not just what keeps us moving forward. It's what gives us reason to exist.

This is when being a doctor hurts the most. When all your knowledge and effort hit a wall. When your patient stops being "a patient" and starts to feel like family. Dan wasn't just someone I cared for. He was someone I cared about. And now, sitting across from me, he said it: "I no longer feel relevant."

He was a retired professor, a husband, a father, a man whose voice once commanded rooms filled with eager minds. His students had admired him, built their own paths from the foundation of his words. He had lived a life of intellect, structure, purpose. And yet, here he was, sitting in front of me, swollen, yellowed, exhausted, and defeated, his breath shallow, his confidence shaken. The once articulate man who taught others to argue their truth could now barely summon the strength to speak his own.

I wanted to tell him he mattered. That he was still relevant to me, to Clara, to the students who still remembered his stories, to the world that had been shaped in some small way by his existence. But even as I opened my mouth, I knew that wasn't the kind of reassurance he needed. What he was really asking wasn't *"Do I matter to you?"* It was *"Do I still matter at all?"*

When the titles and roles that once defined us, husband, professor, provider, expert, begin to fall away, something deeper starts to tremble. The ego panics, searching for a mirror that will reflect who we once were. I could feel Dan's fear because I recognized it. If I am no longer that, then who am I?

I've asked myself the same question more times than I care to admit. I'm a doctor, a mother, a wife, roles that have given my life meaning and direction. But what happens when those roles change or fade? When my hands can no longer hold a stethoscope, when my daughters no longer need me in the same way, when the noise of doing quiets and only *being* remains?

It's a terrifying thought, this idea that our worth might vanish when our usefulness does. But maybe that's where the real work of life begins; learning to see ourselves not by what we produce, but by what we *are*.

"The ego fears loss of identity. But who you are is deeper than any identity. Presence doesn't retire, weaken, or fade. It simply is."
— *Eckhart Tolle*

In that quiet exam room, surrounded by the hum of machines and the scent of antiseptic, I realized that relevance, the sense of being seen, needed, and valued, is not a thing the world gives us. It's something we cultivate from within. Dan was searching for proof that his existence still held meaning, and in truth, so was I.

Dan ended up in the hospital again, his third admission in just a few months. His body was tired. His blood counts had dropped so low that he needed transfusions just to keep going. More tests. The same tests repeated again and again. Each time, we hoped for an answer that never came. I called his specialists, voices blending together in a loop of uncertainty: hematology, cardiology, nephrology, gastroenterology, rheumatology. I even sent him to an academic center, hoping fresh eyes might see what we had missed.

Nothing. Absolutely fucking nothing.

And that's the part of medicine that still brings me to my knees, the helplessness. For all our science, our data, our algorithms and advancements, sometimes it feels like we haven't come that far at all. We circle the unknown like pilgrims, reverent and desperate. In those moments, I question the point of it all. What is the purpose of this journey if it ends in confusion, indignity, and loneliness?

Eventually, I did find the answer. I remember the rush that surged through me — that rare, intoxicating blend of relief and triumph that every clinician chases. For a brief moment, I felt the familiar high of medicine: the belief that I had saved a life. But that victory wasn't mine alone. It came from connection — from a web of communication and collaboration that stretched across colleagues, labs, and late-night messages. The medical team that worked alongside me shared in that discovery. It was through our conversations, our willingness to challenge one another, and my own restless thinking, reading, and listening to Dan himself, that the truth finally surfaced.

Still, by the time we found it, the journey had already changed him. The man who once measured his worth through intellect, precision, and mastery had been reduced to something more elemental. His confidence had eroded, his sharpness dulled by exhaustion and fear. The weight of illness had stripped him of certainty, leaving behind a quieter, more fragile version of himself. I found myself wondering how he would rebuild, what relevance would mean to him now, after coming so close to dying. Perhaps this was his chance to redefine it, to discover what truly mattered when everything else had been taken away.

Watching him, I realized that relevance isn't something we lose because of illness or age. It's something we redefine. When the body weakens, when titles fade, when certainty collapses, relevance shifts from *what we do* to *who we are*, and how we love, and how we're loved in return.

And I think that's what Dan was trying to teach me, without ever intending to. That meaning is not created in diagnosis or success, but in endurance, in the willingness to keep showing up for one another, even when everything else is failing.

I also hoped that our efforts to save his life, demonstrated how relevant he truly was. Now he needed to rediscover relevance within himself.

I was grateful that he didn't have to return to the hospital, grateful that we had found an answer before he became trapped again in that cycle of admissions and discharges. Hospitals are not easy places to navigate. They are no longer what they were meant to be. The system has changed, and not for the better.

***

This is what a hospitalization really looks like:

A patient waits all day to be seen. They can't remember if anyone actually came. Their dignity slowly erodes. They need help to be repositioned. They need a bedpan. But no one comes in time. They soil the bed and lie there until someone arrives. Nutrition services drop off a tray of food, but the room smells like feces. And now the nurses worry the patient isn't eating. But who can eat while lying in their own waste? Hours go by. No one explains what's happening. Pain medication is delayed. Confusion deepens. The day turns into night, and the patient lies there, in pain, hungry, dirty, disoriented. Delirium sets in. Mortality risk climbs. The hospitalization stretches on, and dignity slips further away.

And relevance? Relevance disappears in that bed. When you are no longer a professor, or a parent, or a husband, but just a room number. Not because you have no worth, but because the system has forgotten how to see it.

Here is the truth about that system, at least from where I stand as a physician who has worked in the hospital, in the clinic, and alongside administrators. People often assume that nonprofit hospitals are somehow purer or more benevolent, but in reality, the distinction is largely about taxation, not mission. Both nonprofit and for-profit systems compete in the same markets, charge similar rates, and often operate with the same corporate mindset. Nonprofits may not pay taxes, but their executives still earn millions, and the financial pressures to grow, acquire, and dominate are no different. The label doesn't define the soul of the organization, its leadership does.

Hospitals today are often run by people who do not understand patients. The best hospitals, the ones with the best outcomes, are led by physicians who understand both medicine and management. But too often, the people making the decisions only know spreadsheets. They see numbers, not people. Budgets, not lives.

And yet, within these same systems, there are good people doing their best to hold it all together. Nurses working double shifts, short staffed and stretched thin. Doctors who stay long after their shifts end, trying to make sure no patient is left unseen. Technicians, aides, and staff who show up every day because they care. We do this work because we believe in caring for others, because it still matters to us.

That is why it cuts so deeply when people accuse us of not caring, of being in it for profit, of pushing vaccines or treatments for gain. It's disheartening to watch misinformation spread faster than truth; to see fear and distrust undermine the very thing we have devoted our lives to. We are not perfect, but the vast majority of us entered medicine out of love and a desire to help.

What's most painful is that we are now being attacked from every side. We face pressure from the system that measures success in numbers and profit margins, from administrators who rarely touch a patient, from a government that changes policies faster than we can keep up, and from the very people we are trying to protect. The weight of that constant scrutiny and hostility wears down even the most dedicated among us.

In the end, I had to make a choice. I left the system and began practicing in a concierge setting because I needed to care for patients on my own terms. I needed the freedom to spend time with them, to listen, to think, and to advocate without a timer ticking in the background. It wasn't about exclusivity or privilege, it was about preservation, both theirs and mine. I couldn't keep practicing medicine in a way that demanded I see patients like tasks on a list rather than lives in front of me.

Even now, there are moments of guilt. I know I can only do so much, only care for so many. But I also know that the care I give now is the kind that feels right, that honors the kind of medicine I was trained to practice. I am grateful every day for my patients, for their trust, their patience, and their willingness to walk this path with me. They remind me that relevance isn't about scale or systems; it's about connection, presence, and the impact we have, one person at a time.

Even before I left the system, I think part of me always knew I would. The seed was planted early on, long before I had the courage to walk away.

One of my earliest encounters with this truth came during a job interview which I briefly mentioned earlier. The CEO who had asked me where I saw myself in five years. I told him, honestly, that I wanted to be in leadership, to help improve how health systems function, to make them more compassionate, more efficient, more human. He leaned back, folded his hands, and said, "The problem with you doctors is that you all think you know how to fix the system, but you don't understand business. You should just focus on taking care of patients and leave the rest to us."

His words stayed with me for years. At the time, I was angry, not because he was entirely wrong, but because of how deeply his statement reflected what was broken. He didn't see that doctors *are* the system, that we are the ones who live its consequences alongside our patients. We understand the human cost of every policy, every budget cut, every missed staffing position. To separate care from business is to forget that healthcare is not a product; it is a human exchange.

Years later, I realize that conversation was my first glimpse into the widening gap between medicine and humanity. The administrators would run the numbers, and the clinicians would clean up the damage. It was never meant to be this way. But it taught me something essential, that if I wanted to preserve the heart of what medicine was meant to be, I would have to step outside of the system to do it.

That's what ultimately led me here, to a place where I could practice medicine on my own terms. Concierge care gave me space to breathe again, to think, to listen, to connect. I can no longer help everyone, and I still wrestle with that guilt, but at least

I know the help I do give is real, unhurried, and true to what I believe medicine should be.

That was it. I knew I could not work there. My husband had been considering a job at the same hospital, and as soon as I walked out of that interview, I called him and said, "We need to run." And we did. At first, I was furious. The arrogance of that CEO stayed with me. But over time, I began to see it differently. In some strange way, I am thankful to him. It was the first time I realized how confidently wrong a man in power could be, and how deeply the system had lost its way.

It was also the beginning of a shift in me. Not long after, I accepted another job that was a good one. In that position, I had the opportunity to expand on my love of geriatrics, a stable position, incredible colleagues, and room to grow. But something had changed in me after that interview. His words kept echoing. I started to see the system more clearly, the hierarchy, the bureaucracy, the layers of nonsense that distracted from what really mattered. I began to notice how meetings focused on numbers instead of people, how decisions were made by those far removed from patients, and how good doctors and nurses were burning out under impossible expectations.

That CEO, in his ignorance, gave me the gift of clarity, and I am thankful for that. He helped me see that I did not want to be part of a system that prized compliance over compassion. I wanted to practice medicine the way I believed it was meant to be practiced, rooted in connection, honesty, and presence. It was the start of me finding my own path, one where relevance was no longer defined by titles or institutions, but by how I showed up for people, and the kind of doctor and human being I chose to be.

All of it stayed with me, even as the years went by and my career evolved. I truly loved my job and the people I worked with, but I was starting to butt heads with the system itself. I had also been in business school, working toward my master's in business administration with a focus on healthcare administration, and by the time I finished, the clarity had started to set in. I wanted to grow, to be something more, to lead and to create change. But at my core, I was a doctor. My sense of relevance came from the connection I had with my patients, not from the meetings or the administrative titles. Still, a part of me hoped that by doing something different, by stepping into leadership, maybe I could help others see that there was another way to practice medicine, another way to care.

***

I thought about all of this again in the thick of my uncle's illness. My mother and I flew to Salt Lake City to visit him. I pushed her in a wheelchair through the airport, boarding slowly. Her gait was unsteady, her strength no longer what it once was. Yet as I watched her, I remembered the woman who once navigated international travel alone with two daughters in tow, my sister and me, through unfamiliar airports in a country whose language she didn't even speak. And still, she kept us safe. Her presence was steady, her intuition sharp. She was our protector. And now, years later, I was hers, making sure she was fed, comfortable, and at ease. The roles had shifted, as they do with time, but the strength remained, only now it lived in a different form.

When we arrived, we spent a few days with my uncle, aunt, and visited cousins. My uncle wasn't eating the way he used to. He wasn't talking the way he used to. He sat on the couch quietly next to my mother, and I saw how physically small they both were. Frail. Different. And yet, still here. Still relevant. Still part of the story. Even though their bodies had weakened, there was something deeply grounded about them. They were still rooted, connected to life and to each other in a way that went beyond the physical. Watching them reminded me of the quiet strength that comes with age, the kind that doesn't need to prove anything. It simply exists.

That moment made me think of why we named our practice *Golden Oak Medicine*. The "golden" for the golden years, a stage of life that holds so much wisdom and light, and the "oak" for the deep roots that keep us connected, steady, and alive even as the seasons change. My mother and uncle embodied that spirit completely. Though time had reshaped them, their presence still carried weight, like old trees whose roots run deep beneath the surface, reminding me that relevance has nothing to do with appearance or strength, but everything to do with being grounded in who you are and what you've given to the world.

As a little girl, these were my giants. My mother with her fierce love. My uncle with his mythic stories, how he helped students escape post-revolution Iran, carried the Olympic torch in 2002, had a photo with Margaret Thatcher on the wall. I don't know every part of his story. He once told me, "To give you the good, I'd have to give you the skeletons too." Still, I know this: he helped everyone. And now, life had narrowed. The world he once moved through so powerfully had become smaller. But this shrinking wasn't failure. It was closure.

What if aging isn't a falling apart, but a coming back together? What if our lives are meant to grow, and then slowly, sacredly, return to center? If we're lucky, we live long enough to shrink before we go. We get to pass the torch gently, instead of leaving chaos behind. Life, in its quiet wisdom, gives us the chance to return to the essence of who we are, stripped of titles and roles, so that we can remember what truly matters. In that way, aging is not a loss, but a homecoming, a gathering of all the versions of ourselves we've ever been, brought back into one body, one presence, before we release it all.

Yet we resist this. Our culture doesn't honor the beauty of that return. My older patients struggle, not because they are weak, but because no one taught them that this is part of the journey. We never prepared them for aging, for decline, for death. No one shows us how, and how would they? Even we, as physicians, are trained to fight aging rather than walk beside it. No one tells us that growing old is not a failure of the body but a triumph of time, proof that we have lived long enough to witness the full arc of our story.

***

We spend our lives building, achieving, doing, and so little time learning how to let go. Our society worships youth, speed, and productivity, convincing us that to be relevant we must always be useful, visible, and strong. So, when our bodies begin to change, when strength fades and reflection takes the place of ambition, we panic. We equate slowing down with disappearing, as though meaning only matters when it can be seen. But relevance should never have been about the outside. It has always lived in the quiet constancy of who we are, in the wisdom we pass on, in the love we give, and in the lives we've shaped along the way. So many of my patients sit in front of me, not just in physical pain, but in emotional distress. "I used to run every morning," they tell me. "I used to be able to walk without stopping. Now I get short of breath. Now I'm tired all the time." Their bodies, once strong and agile, no longer obey in the same way, and the result is often panic, sadness, even depression. The anxiety shows up as dizziness, chest discomfort, fatigue, but underneath it all is something deeper, the quiet grief of becoming a different version of themselves.

It is not just about breathlessness or physical weakness; it is about relevance. It is about identity. It is about mourning the person they once were and struggling to understand who they are now. I can see it in their eyes, the disbelief, the frustration, the sense of betrayal by their own bodies. They are not simply mourning strength or stamina; they are mourning the certainty that their lives still hold the same value. No one prepared them for this shift. No one told them that meaning doesn't end when youth does, that purpose can evolve, that being is enough. And so, they sit across from me, searching for answers that medicine alone cannot give, when what they really need is permission to still matter.

What I've come to see is that peace comes when we stop comparing who we are now to who we once were. Aging doesn't make us lesser; it transforms us into something quieter, deeper, and often wiser. But no one teaches us how to live in that space. We are told that worth is tied to youth, to speed, to visible achievement. We are taught to move, to do, to produce, never to simply be. No one ever tells us that stillness can hold just as much value, that being here, alive and aware, is enough. And I'll be honest—I struggle with this myself.

***

In November of 2024, I had both of my hips replaced at age 45 due to congenital hip dysplasia. For two years leading up to surgery, I couldn't sleep through the night. I'd be jolted awake in pain, unable to walk comfortably during the day, let alone enjoy hiking or chasing after my kids. I limped around my office. My patients would often express sympathy. I had such severe instability that during a camping trip to Iceland with my husband, I fell in a campground shower, sustained a concussion, and broke my four front teeth. I needed emergency dental work while abroad. Later, four of those teeth died. I felt broken. I was grieving, not just the loss of mobility, but the loss of control.

But somewhere amid the sadness, I also found gratitude. Grateful that I could get help. Grateful that I could walk again. Both hips were in such bad shape that I didn't even know which one to replace first. So I did both. Ten days after surgery, I was back at work. I walked the hospital halls I used to dread navigating. I was sore. But I was no longer in the same pain.

Yes, I now live with certain limitations. But I've learned to honor what I can do, instead of mourning what I can't. That's what my patients teach me over and over again, if we surrender to the now, we find new strength. Not in returning to what we were, but in discovering who we are now.

"Whatever the present moment contains, accept it as if you had chosen it."
—Eckhart Tolle

That kind of surrender takes work. Despite everything I know, despite all the lessons I've learned from my patients, I still find myself grieving what my body could once do. There are days I feel the shift in energy, in endurance, in capacity, and I have to consciously remind myself: This is part of it. This is the path. Life expands, and then it contracts. Not as punishment, but as a natural rhythm. A return to center. A soft closing of the circle.

Spiritual and religious beliefs vary. What we think happens next shapes how we live now. But no matter what you believe, we all deserve preparation. We deserve the dignity of knowing this stage of life is not a loss of relevance. It's a distillation of it.

Arthur reminded me of that. He came in after his beloved partner, June, had passed. For months, June had been sick. He'd taken her to the hospital again and again. And finally, they made the decision to bring in hospice.

To shift from fixing to feeling. From doing to being. As he sat in my office, he told me how hard it was, how he didn't think he'd survive much longer without her. That he had always believed he would go soon after she did. That their lives had been so intertwined, he didn't see how he'd carry on. But June had told him something before she died. Something simple. Something that stayed with him. "You may be needed." And now, as he moves through his grief, he returns to those words.

"You may be needed."

He shows up for others. He is building to give back; he is taking classes. He brings joy to his friends. He tells her story. He breathes.

We all need to hear that.
You are still needed.
You are still relevant.
You always were.

Chapter 11

The Full Circle and the Big Picture

I am who I am because I strive to embrace the world with open eyes and a listening heart.

As we approach the end of this journey, it feels important to pause and reflect on what this book is truly about, and who it is for. These pages were written for anyone searching for meaning in the midst of life's uncertainty, for those who have loved deeply, lost deeply, and are still trying to make sense of what it all means. The lessons within were not born of theory or research alone, but through years of sitting beside my patients, listening to their stories, and witnessing the extraordinary wisdom that lives within ordinary lives.

Each chapter has been a thread in the tapestry of this human experience—woven with love, loss, resilience, relevance, and acceptance woven from the countless interactions that have shaped me as both a physician and a person. The threads are not just connections; they are lifelines, reminders that meaning is found not in isolation but in relationship. My patients have been my teachers. Through them, I have learned what it means to live with intention, to find strength in vulnerability, and to embrace aging not as an ending, but as a return to truth.

And I must admit, I am not immune to chaos. My mind races: I am driven and restless. There are days when I cry without warning, when I lose sleep chasing ideas, when my thoughts collide faster than I can't organize them. I get angry. I lose my way. I am, at times, a ball of fire, burning, then flickering, then burning again. But my patients, these remarkable souls, have a way of bringing me back. Their steadiness, their perspective, their acceptance of life as it is, remind me to slow down and breathe. They ground me in the present moment, reminding me that meaning doesn't live in perfection, but in presence.

In a world that moves too quickly and values productivity over presence, I want this book to be a gentle call to action. Learn from those who came before you. Sit with your elders. Listen to their stories. Notice the quiet ways they have endured, loved, adapted, and forgiven. Through them, you will learn not only how to appreciate life, but how to live it, deeply, meaningfully, and with gratitude for every fleeting moment.

The Wisdom of Elders

We must actively seek out our elders, not merely to hear their stories, but to truly *listen* to them, to understand what life has taught them, and what they can still teach us. Their lives are filled with hard-earned wisdom about resilience, love, loss, and the very essence of what it means to be human. These are not just stories from the past; they are living testaments, guiding lights that illuminate the paths we walk now. When we ask them to share, we are not just honoring their history, we are preserving the map of who we are and who we might become. Their voices are like mirrors, reflecting both our potential and our fragility, reminding us that every stage of life has meaning and purpose.

In my own life, the lessons I've learned from my patients have been both humbling and transformative. I came to medicine thinking I would be the one teaching, diagnosing, fixing. But again and again, they became my teachers. So many of them have faced loss, illness, and uncertainty with a grace that left me quiet inside. They taught me that true strength isn't loud, it doesn't look like control or perfection. It looks like acceptance. It looks like a trembling hand still reaching out for another, even when everything hurts. It looks like the courage to keep showing up, not because you have answers, but because you still have love to give.

I've watched patients grieve the loss of spouses, children, and independence, yet still find meaning in connection, in memory, and in the smallest rituals of daily life, a morning coffee, a shared laugh, a familiar song. Their quiet endurance taught me that the fragility of life is not a reason to despair, but an invitation to notice, to savor, to live with intention. These moments with them were never just about bearing witness to suffering; they were lessons in how to live, fully, compassionately, and without fear of impermanence.

Even in the final stages of life, my patients have revealed to me the profound strength that can exist within vulnerability. Again and again, I have sat beside people who, even as they faced death, were willing to share their fears, their regrets, and their hopes. Their honesty has changed me. It reminded me that vulnerability is not weakness, it is the purest form of courage. It is the willingness to be seen, exactly as we are, even when time is running out.

Their lives and deaths have become a kind of compass for me, a grounding force that pulls me back whenever I lose my way. In their stories, I see the full circle of humanity, what it means to live, to love, to let go, and to return again to what is most essential: connection.

The Fragility of Life

Before we can fully understand the depth of love, we must first face the truth of life's fragility. Every moment we live exists on borrowed time, and yet most of us move through our days as if the supply is endless. This book began with that very truth, the recognition that life is as delicate as it is magnificent, that in one heartbeat everything we know can change. The fragility of life is not meant to frighten us, but to awaken us. It calls us to presence, to gratitude, to the sacredness of being alive in this fleeting, imperfect form.

Throughout this journey, we've witnessed how easily everything can shift — with an illness, an accident, a diagnosis, a goodbye. But it is within that uncertainty that meaning takes root. Fragility teaches us to live with intention, to slow down, to notice. It reminds us that what is temporary is not trivial; it is sacred precisely because it will not last.

My own experience with James remains the compass that

points me toward this truth. His brief but luminous life changed everything about how I see the world. In his eight weeks on this earth, he taught me what decades of living could not, that love is the only thing strong enough to hold both joy and sorrow in the same space. His life, and his death, shattered the illusion of permanence and showed me that even when something ends, the love that was born from it endures. That love becomes the bridge between what was and what remains.

This understanding of life's fragility has shaped how I approach everything, medicine, family, friendship, even the way I look at a sunrise. It has taught me to hold people a little longer, to speak more gently, to live with fewer guarantees and more grace. I've learned that control is an illusion, but connection is real. And in a world that constantly rushes toward the next thing, the greatest act of courage may be to pause and truly be here, now.

We cannot control the length of our lives, but we can shape their depth. The fragility of life is not a limitation; it is an invitation, to live more fully, love more freely, forgive more easily, and show up for one another while we still can. It asks us to stop waiting for the right moment and to realize that this, right now, *is* the moment.

When we embrace that truth, we begin to understand love not as something to be earned or kept, but as something to be lived, freely, courageously, and without hesitation. That is where the next part of the story begins.

The Role of Love

Jas's unwavering support during our grief over James revealed the truest nature of love. His quiet strength, his steadfastness even as he carried his own sorrow, showed me that love is not merely about sharing joy, but about holding each other through pain. It is the hand that steadies you when your world falls apart, the voice that says, "I am still here," even when words no longer help. Through him, I learned that love is not fragile. It is not easily broken. It is the most enduring force we will ever know.

In the weeks and months after James's death, there were moments when I felt completely lost. My mind was chaos, my body hollowed out by grief, and yet, Jas remained my constant. He was my mirror, my anchor, and my reminder that even when everything else collapses, love remains. His presence wasn't about fixing or reassuring, it was about *being*. That is what love does. It endures. It witnesses. It holds. Through that experience, I came to see love as something far greater than emotion. Love is energy. It is movement. It is the force that gives meaning to the fragile span between birth and death. It connects us to one another, to the divine, to the mystery that breathes through everything alive. When we "choose love," we are choosing presence over distance, compassion over pride, and connection over fear.

Every faith tradition, in its own way, centers love at the heart of human existence. In Christianity, love is both commandment and grace, *"Love one another, as I have loved you."* In Buddhism, love is expressed as *metta*, loving-kindness, an active compassion that extends even to those who harm us. In Islam, *Rahma*, divine mercy, is rooted in love, a reminder that every act of care is a reflection of God's compassion. And even beyond religion, philosophers, poets, and scientists all circle back to this same truth: love is the fabric that holds the universe together.

We spend so much of our lives chasing relevance, success, and security, forgetting that all of it begins and ends in love. It is love that gives our stories meaning. It is love that softens grief and transforms loss into connection. It is love that teaches us forgiveness and humility.

In navigating our grief, Jas and I found a rhythm again, not through words, but through being. There were days when we said nothing, and yet everything was said. Love filled the silence. It gave us the courage to rise, to parent, to heal, and eventually to find joy again. Our journey through sorrow revealed that love is not a fleeting emotion or a perfect story; it is a lifelong practice of showing up, again and again, even when it hurts.

And I'll admit, I don't always get it right. I am human. I stumble, I falter, I lose my patience. There are days I want to retreat, to turn inward, to stop trying. But love is what brings me back. I will try to show up. I will plan to show up. And even when I don't, the intention remains, the quiet, imperfect commitment to keep moving toward connection, toward presence, toward love. Because the journey never really ends. It just keeps unfolding, one act of showing up at a time.

Love is what makes us human. Love is what makes us whole. And when everything else fades, titles, youth, ambition, it is love that remains, the pulse that connects us back to one another, and to whatever waits beyond this life.

The In-Between Moments

Reflecting on the in-between moments of life, those quiet spaces between milestones and endings, has reminded me of what truly gives our lives meaning. It is not only the great triumphs or tragedies that define us, but the subtle, often overlooked intervals in between. These are the moments that shape us, that teach us how to love, to forgive, to endure, and to begin again. The in-between is where we grow, where we learn to sit with uncertainty and still find beauty in the ordinary.

Our experiences with patients, family, and personal loss have revealed just how sacred those in-between moments can be. Each conversation, each shared silence, each small act of care becomes part of the greater story. They may not be the moments we post or celebrate, but they are the ones that hold the deepest truths. These quiet spaces teach us that purpose is not always found in what we achieve, but in how we *exist*, how we show up for others and for ourselves when no one is watching.

In my work with patients, I've seen how profoundly these moments matter. A hand held during fear, a smile exchanged in the midst of illness, a shared laugh that momentarily lightens the weight of suffering, these simple gestures often mean more than the grandest interventions. I've learned that medicine, like life, happens in the pauses. Healing begins not only in treatments, but in presence. In being there.

When I think about it now, it's clear that the in-between is where love resides. It's where relevance is born. It's where adaptation happens quietly, without ceremony. These intervals, between health and illness, joy and sorrow, youth and age, are not gaps to be endured, but gifts to be lived. They remind us that our lives are not defined by beginnings or endings, but by everything that unfolds in between.

The in-between moments are where we meet ourselves most honestly. They are where we learn to see the sacred in the ordinary, to hold both joy and pain at once, to keep loving even when we are uncertain. When we honor these moments, we honor the wholeness of life itself.

Transparency and Honesty

As I reflect on the arc of this journey, aging, caregiving, love, and loss, transparency and honesty continue to emerge not only as principles for medicine, but as essential companions for living and dying well. Earlier in this book, I wrote about how truth strengthens the bond between physician and patient. But now, through the lens of aging and relevance, I see transparency as something far more profound: a way to preserve dignity, to foster connection, and to live with integrity in our final chapters.

Aging brings change, physical, emotional, and spiritual. There is often a temptation, in ourselves and in those who love us, to soften the truth or look away from decline. But real peace comes from clarity. Whether it's a conversation about care preferences, a difficult admission of fear, or an unspoken acknowledgment that time is shifting, honesty creates room for presence. It allows us to live, and to die, with intention.

Yet the need for truth extends far beyond the walls of medicine. I often wonder why leaders, political, corporate, and even spiritual, hesitate to speak truth. Why do we guard information, conceal reality, or twist words out of fear of consequence or loss of control? What if truth-telling, no matter how uncomfortable, could actually prevent the very suffering we try to avoid, death, loss, war, division? The same way dishonesty fractures trust between patient and physician, it fractures societies, families, and nations.

Transparency, when practiced with compassion, has the power to heal at every level of human experience. It bridges the gap between misunderstanding and empathy, between fear and trust. Truth is not a weapon; it is a light. And even when it exposes pain, it also reveals the path toward peace.

But I've also learned that transparency is not only about grand acts of honesty. Sometimes it's simply about *speaking up*. It's choosing not to remain silent when something matters. It's finding the courage to express your truth, not to wound, but to be seen. I have to remind myself of that constantly. There are times I hold back to protect others, to keep peace, to avoid conflict. But silence, when born from fear, can be its own kind of dishonesty. Speaking up with kindness, with clarity, with love, is its own form of healing.

In my life and in my practice, I've come to see that transparency is not about control, it's about freedom. It's the freedom to say what we need, what we fear, and what we hope for without shame. It's the freedom to face uncertainty with courage instead of denial. Transparency invites us to lay down the heavy armor of pretense and show up as we are, vulnerable, imperfect, real.

I've watched my patients, and my own family, navigate these transitions. I've seen how truth, though sometimes piercing, can be profoundly grounding. The most beautiful goodbyes I've witnessed were not marked by perfection, but by honesty, words spoken without filters, feelings shared without fear, and love expressed without hesitation. And that, to me, is the quiet power of transparency. It is not simply about medical accuracy or ethical precision. It is about liberation. When we choose truth, we release ourselves from illusion. When we speak truth, we honor life exactly as it is, fragile, fleeting, and undeniably beautiful.

But I will admit, I am still learning this. I stumble, I retreat, I choose silence when I should speak. There are moments when fear or pride gets in the way, when I worry about being misunderstood, or when my own emotions cloud the clarity I hope to bring. I am human, chaotic, fiery, emotional, and I keep trying to find balance between honesty and grace. Some days I get it right. Other days I do not. But each time I return to this truth: that transparency, even imperfectly practiced, draws me closer to peace. It reminds me that vulnerability is not weakness, it is the truest form of courage.

Compassion as a Guiding Force

Compassion, too, emerges as a guiding force, especially during the in-between moments that shape our experiences. It is in these everyday interactions and ordinary challenges that compassion reveals its true power. By approaching others with empathy and kindness, we create a supportive environment where people feel valued and understood. Compassion is more than a response to significant events; it is a continuous practice of acknowledging and easing the struggles of those around us.

In my practice, compassion is a cornerstone of my approach to patient care. It involves not only addressing physical symptoms but also recognizing and responding to the emotional and psychological needs of my patients. By approaching each patient with empathy and understanding, I am able to provide more comprehensive and compassionate care that addresses their overall well-being.

Similarly, in our daily lives, compassion allows us to connect with others on a deeper level and to offer genuine support in times of need. Whether through small acts of kindness, words of encouragement, or simply showing up and listening, compassion transforms ordinary interactions into moments of meaning. Compassion, when practiced fully, becomes the doorway to empathy. It invites us to step outside of ourselves and into another's experience, not just to acknowledge their pain, but to *feel* it, to sense what life might be like in their world.

At its root, empathy is the emotional extension of compassion. It's what happens when care moves from the heart into the body, when understanding becomes feeling. It is the pause that says, *I see you, and I'm willing to stand beside you in this.*

For me, this has always come naturally with my patients. I can sit with their fears, their pain, their stories, and find patience and clarity. Yet I've realized that I often struggle to extend that same grace to the people closest to me. With my family, my emotions can run hotter; I interrupt, I rush, I assume. It's easier to listen to a stranger than to someone whose history is intertwined with my own. I'm still learning that compassion and empathy don't require fixing or teaching, they require presence. They ask us to listen, really listen, without judgment or defensiveness.

Over the years, my patients have taught me this lesson

more than anyone else. I've heard their deepest fears, dreams, and regrets. So many have told me that what they wished for most was more time, not just time to live, but time to truly connect. They wished they had listened more, loved more, been more present with the people who mattered most. Those confessions stay with me. They remind me that compassion and empathy are not just virtues to practice in medicine, but ways of being that shape how we love, how we forgive, and how we find meaning in the lives intertwined with our own.

Creating a Fulfilling Life

I don't write these words as an expert. I write them as a student of life, still learning, still stumbling, still asking questions, still failing. Everything I've shared in these pages comes not from certainty, but from experience, time spent listening to my patients, my elders, my own family, and the quiet voice that surfaces when life slows down long enough to be heard. Gathering their stories. These thoughts are not conclusions, they are reflections. They are the lessons I've gathered from those who have lived longer, loved harder, and suffered more deeply than I have.

What does it really mean to create a fulfilling life? So many people talk about happiness as though it were a destination, but I think it's more like a landscape—one that we build and rebuild through the choices we make, the love we give, and the meaning we create. I think about my own life often. Am I happy with where I am? Do I have regrets? Have I crafted the life I truly want?

Not long ago, I was walking through a park in Asheville on a cool fall day. The trees were turning, the brilliant reds, golds, and yellows that make the mountains feel alive. The air was crisp, the light soft, the ground carpeted in leaves that glowed like embers. I turned to my friend and said, "I am so thankful. Every decision I've made, every joy and mistake and heartbreak, has brought me to this moment." I think of that often. When things are hard, when life feels uncertain, I remind myself that I created this path. I chose it. And I am grateful for it.

When it comes to creating a fulfilling life, I've learned that true satisfaction comes from crafting your own path—not one that others expect of you, but one that aligns with your values, your voice, your truth. Fulfillment is not a prize handed out for perfection. It's the quiet contentment that comes from living in harmony with who you are. Success and peace come when we stop chasing the external and start tending to what is internal.

This way of living requires resilience, because it means you must listen to yourself even when the world is loud. But that inner alignment, rooted in authenticity, creates the foundation for a meaningful life. When we choose to live this way, we discover that happiness is not about having everything, it's about loving what we have, and recognizing that even the hardest moments have shaped us into who we were meant to become.

Triumph, Strength, and Hope

Triumph, strength, and hope are powerful forces that emerge from our experiences and quietly shape how we move through life. They are not distant ideals or lofty virtues reserved for the extraordinary; they are the everyday companions that guide us through hardship, uncertainty, and change. When we embrace them, we learn to face adversity with courage, to find meaning within our struggles, and to cultivate a sense of hope that propels us forward even when the path is unclear.

Throughout my life and career, I have seen these values reflected again and again, in my patients, my family, and within myself. Triumph doesn't always look like victory. It is often quiet, unseen, unfolding in the moments when someone chooses to rise after being knocked down, or finds peace in a reality they cannot change. Strength is not the absence of fear or pain; it is the steady willingness to face both with grace. And hope, the most fragile and yet most enduring of the three, is what allows us to keep moving even when the future feels uncertain.

I have used the word *resilience* more times than I can count. It's a word that followed me through residency, one that appears in every medical conference, leadership retreat, and professional burnout talk. But with time, I've realized that resilience is not a single skill, it is a composite of triumph, strength, and hope. It is the ability to endure, to bend without breaking, to keep believing that something meaningful can still be built from what was lost.

If my patients have taught me anything, it is that they have *triumphed* over life itself. I sometimes joke with them that Mother Nature is trying to kill us off, that once we have reproduced and raised our young, she considers her job done. And yet, here they are, proving her wrong every day. They are living longer, fuller, more purposeful lives than ever before. They are redefining what it means to age, to remain relevant, to keep showing up for life even when it becomes more fragile.

Like Dr. Louise Aronson describes so beautifully in *Elderhood*, this final third of life is not a slow fading, it is a continuation of becoming. My patients embody that truth. They show me that it takes extraordinary power to grow old. Not giving up, not withdrawing, but adapting to every new phase. That is strength. That is triumph.

Every wrinkle, every scar, every story is a mark of endurance. Aging is not failure; it is evidence of survival. It takes immense courage to face each morning with a body that no longer obeys as it once did, and to still choose joy, gratitude, and connection. That is what my patients do. That is what they teach me.

To live long enough to become an elder is to have defied the odds. To live those years with purpose, humility, humor, and grace, that is triumph. That is strength. That is hope.

The Full Circle of Life

Ultimately, life is a full circle, encompassing the entirety of our existence, from joy to sorrow, birth to death, and everything in between. Each moment, whether radiant or painful, belongs to the same continuum. By embracing the full spectrum of our experiences and reflecting on the lessons they bring, we begin to see that nothing is wasted. Every joy, every loss, every act of courage and grace shapes us into who we are meant to become.

When we allow ourselves to see the full picture, we recognize the profound interconnectedness of all things. Our stories are not isolated but woven together with those of others, forming a vast tapestry of human experience. The choices we make, the people we love, the suffering we endure, and the compassion we offer are all threads within that design. Each moment, each decision, each breath contributes to the greater pattern.

We are no more special than the next person we encounter, no more extraordinary than the stranger passing by. Each of us was born into different circumstances, some into abundance, others into scarcity. Some were given opportunities, others created them out of nothing. Yet, within this circle, what defines us is not what we start with, but what we create along the way. How we choose to live, to love, to think, and to act within this brief and wondrous journey, that is the measure of a life.

How we meet sorrow, loss, and pain, how we hold joy and gratitude, how we forgive, and how we begin again, this is the essence of the circle. This is what completes it. From the earth we rise, and to the earth we return. The circle closes, and everything in between is what we have created: the love we've given, the lives we've touched, the meaning we've made.

To embrace the full circle of life is to honor the depth and complexity of our shared journey. It is to see that the purpose of life is not to outshine others but to walk beside them, to love and be loved, to leave the world a little gentler for our having been here. Each moment, each relationship, each act of kindness contributes to the richness of our existence, helping us move through this world with greater clarity, peace, and purpose.

And at the heart of this circle is love. It is the one truth that transcends every boundary, cultural, spiritual, and temporal. Love is the language of all faiths, the sacred thread that connects us. In the Gospel of John, Jesus said, *"A new command I give you: Love one another. As I have loved you, so you must love one another."* (John 13:34). It is the simplest and most profound teaching of all.

If we could all live by that, if we could choose love in every word, every gesture, every silence, we might finally understand the meaning of the circle. Life begins with love and ends with love, and everything in between is our chance to practice it.

Relevance

In Chapter Ten, I explored the idea of relevance, the quiet question that so many of my patients ask in the moments between words: *Do I still matter?* Over time, I've come to see that relevance does not disappear with age or illness. It changes form. It sheds the layers of accomplishment and identity we've built around it and returns us to something purer, more enduring. We are not relevant because of what we produce or achieve, but because of who we are, what we've loved, taught, endured, and shared.

Our relevance lives in the echoes of our kindness, in the people we've shaped, and in the love we've left behind. It exists in the smallest gestures: the conversation that soothed someone's fear, the wisdom that sparked courage, the compassion that made another person feel seen. Relevance isn't a spotlight; it's a quiet glow that lingers long after we've moved on.

And yet, this is something I still struggle with. I have to remind myself again and again that my work, my titles, even my role as a physician, do not make up the whole of who I am. They are expressions of me, not the entirety of me. I know, someday, these parts of my identity will fade, my pace will slow, my hands will tremble, my patients will belong to others, and when that day comes, I want to remember that relevance does not end there. It simply transforms.

Aging doesn't erase relevance; it distills it. When the noise of accomplishment quiets, what remains is the essence of being itself. In that stillness, we remember that we mattered, not for what we did, but for how we lived, how we loved, and how we made others feel.

Relevance is not something we earn or hold onto; it's something we recognize in the mirror of our humanity — the quiet knowing that we were always enough.

Epilogue

Lessons from the Elders

In writing this book, my aim has been to honor and reflect the profound lessons I have learned from my elders. Each day, I am privileged to spend time with them, listening to their stories, absorbing their wisdom, and often receiving their heartfelt advice. Through these interactions, I have come to understand that the true value of their experiences lies in our willingness individually and collectively to listen and learn from them.

Embracing the vulnerability of life has been one of the most enduring lessons they've shared. Understanding the delicate nature of our existence reminds me to cherish every moment, to live with intention, and to find beauty in the everyday. This awareness of life's impermanence encourages me to savor the present and to appreciate the fleeting nature of time.

The power of love, as demonstrated through the

unwavering support of loved ones, extends beyond mere affection. It is in the act of standing together through adversity that we truly experience love's strength. This realization has reinforced the importance of nurturing and cherishing our relationships, recognizing that love's true essence lies in its capacity to uplift and sustain us during life's challenges.

In my interactions with elders, I've come to value the moments in between life's grand events. These intervals, often quiet, unremarkable, or overlooked, are where much of life actually happens. They shape our understanding of love and purpose. By embracing these in-between moments, I've learned to find richness and depth in the everyday experiences that often go unnoticed, making each day significant in its own right.

Transparency and honesty foster trust and understanding. The open communication I've witnessed among elders reminds me how clarity and compassion strengthen every relationship. In the context of aging and the end of life, honesty becomes more than a virtue, it becomes a necessity. It creates space for clarity, legacy, and dignity. It allows for meaningful conversations about legacy, dignity, and care, conversations that remind us how important it is to be seen and heard, even in our most vulnerable moments.

Compassion, especially in the midst of everyday struggles, is a guiding force that enriches our connections with others. Through empathy and kindness, we create supportive environments where people feel valued and understood. This practice of compassion is integral to enhancing our relationships and to fostering a sense of community and belonging.

Living a fulfilling life requires us to align with our true selves, embracing our values and desires rather than conforming to external expectations. This alignment, as demonstrated by the elders I've encountered, leads to a sense of purpose and fulfillment that guides us through life's journey. By crafting our own path and pursuing our unique goals, we find satisfaction and meaning in our endeavors.

Triumph, strength, and hope are not separate from courage, they are the very threads that weave it together. Facing adversity with courage and finding meaning in our struggles allow us to move forward even in the darkest times. The lessons learned from those who have faced their own challenges inspire us to approach life with a sense of hope and determination, finding strength in the process of overcoming obstacles.

And more recently, through conversations about what it means to feel relevant, even in the face of aging, loss, or physical decline, I've learned that our presence and purpose do not fade; they evolve. Relevance is not tied to productivity or roles. It's about being seen. It's about connection, legacy, presence. We remain relevant as long as we continue to love, to bear witness, to show up, and to leave even the smallest imprint of care.

The big lesson I have drawn from my observations and experiences is the importance of listening to and learning from the wisdom of our elders. Their lessons, if not heeded, risk being lost and forgotten. This can lead to struggles and hardships that might otherwise be avoided. I have seen this truth reflected in my own life, through my losses, failures, and triumphs.

We have so much to gain by holding space for those who've walked before us. Their stories are not relics; they are maps. Their voices are not echoes of the past; they are guides for the future.

Let us shift our cultural focus to one where our elders are

revered and their wisdom is cherished. By leaving behind an overemphasis on youth and the present, we can create a more inclusive and respectful environment that values the contributions and insights of those who have come before us.

And to the young aspiring doctors out there: consider the field of geriatrics. It's not just a rewarding career; it's the best field of medicine that exists, if only because it's the one where you get to spend the most time with people who've had the chance to master life's best lessons. Embracing their wisdom will not only enrich your practice but might just spare you a few of the rookie mistakes the rest of us had to learn the hard way.

May we all strive to listen more attentively, embrace the lessons of the past, and apply them to enrich our collective human experience, ensuring that their voices continue to guide us in meaningful ways. And maybe, just maybe, that's how we make this fragile life a little more whole.

Last Thoughts

As I write these words, I do so with a full heart, aware of the divisions that now run through our country, the arrogance, the noise, the certainty of those who believe themselves bigger, better, holier. I write not from politics, but from what I've learned sitting beside the dying, from the bedside lessons that strip away illusion and reveal what truly matters. Oh, how I wish I could tell our leaders, those who wield power carelessly, who build walls instead of bridges, that the choices they make, the people they hurt, the greed they justify, will one day return to them. When their bodies are frail and the noise of the world fades, it won't be power or politics they remember. It will be love, or the absence of it. The people they've touched, or the ones they've harmed.

Perhaps the full circle is, in the end, a plea to return to simplicity, to love ourselves, to accept ourselves, and to love one another again. That is the medicine the world needs most.

And as a physician, I cannot separate that truth from the work I do. Medicine belongs to the sacred space between doctor and patient. It does not belong in the hands of politicians, nor in the doctrines of religion. Healthcare is not a battlefield for control, but a covenant of trust. I have my beliefs, I have my truths, but in the exam room, at the bedside, my duty is not to my ideology but to the human being in front of me, to honor their values, their fears, and their faith. That is where medicine belongs: *in compassion, not control; in truth, not judgment; in love, not law.*

Our democracy is sacred. You cannot manipulate it or undermine the stability of this country, the greatness built by those who came before us, the foundation that has held us together through centuries of change. You cannot destroy the Constitution, nor the dreams it was meant to protect. To our leaders, I say this: you are out of touch. You have twisted faith into a tool for gain and preyed on those who trusted you. Shame on you for that. None of us are immune from disease or death. The only thing that will matter, in the end, is how we chose to live, how we chose to touch one another's lives, with kindness, or with harm.

If I have learned anything from a lifetime spent at the intersection of life and death, it is this: the measure of our lives is not found in how loudly we speak, but in how gently we listen; not in how much power we hold, but in how much love we give.

That is the lesson my patients have taught me, and the one I hope this book leaves behind.

The End.

Thank you for reading.

Now go find an elder, listen, learn, and let them teach you the lessons of life.

Acknowledgements

To my husband, Jas — your strength, level-headedness, and unwavering steadiness have carried me through some of the hardest and most meaningful chapters of my life. Your clarity and honesty anchor me in ways I never expected but always needed.

To my three girls — Mila, my eldest, steady and rational beyond her years; Zoey, whose happiness and warmth brighten even my darkest days; and Peyton, whose challenges and triumphs have expanded my understanding of love and patience. You are each a different part of my heart.

To James — your brief life changed me forever. Your presence continues to guide my work, my writing, and the way I practice medicine.

To my parents, who taught me resilience and sacrifice, and to my sister, Golnar, whose love has been a constant source of support — thank you for shaping the woman and mother I am.

To my in-laws, whose love and support have been an anchor in my life — thank you for embracing me as family.

To my Aunt Jan, whose presence changed the course of my life. Without you, I would be writing an entirely different story.

To my patients — thank you for trusting me with your stories, your fears, and your lives. You have taught me more about strength, courage, and love than any textbook ever could. You are woven into every chapter of this book.